MW00563994

Praise for *Employee Resource Group Excellence*

"No one has done more research on ERGs than Robert. He has the deep data, the rich stories, and the proven strategies that gives him unmatched insights into what it takes for ERGs to have transformative impact."

—Andrés Tapia,
Korn Ferry Global DE&I Strategist and co-author, "The 5 Disciplines of Inclusive Leadership."

"Dr. Robert Rodriguez has written a must-read primer for anyone considering an ERG leadership role. Extraordinary insights and guidance! Read this book – and learn from the best in the business."

—Mariana Fagnilli,
Vice President, Global Office of Diversity, Equity & Inclusion, Liberty Mutual Insurance

"You cannot solve what you are not willing to see."

—Tyronne Stoudemire,
Global VP of Diversity, Equity and Inclusion, Co-Chair, Global Diversity, Equity and Inclusion Counsel, Hyatt Hotels Corporation

"Dr. Rodriguez is one of the most established and knowledgeable resources on the strategic imperative of ERGs, quantifying their value and guiding the world's top companies in their journeys towards workplace belonging for all. This book is a must-have resource!"

—Jennifer Brown,
Founder and CEO, Jennifer Brown Consulting; Author, "How to Be an Inclusive Leader: Your Role in Creating Cultures of Belonging Where Everyone Can Thrive."

"A crucial guide to having successful and impactful ERGs, while at the same time, creating an inclusive culture. This book provides strategic steps, metrics, and insights to elevating the performance of employee resource groups."

—Jorge De La Jara,
Senior Director, Pro Customer Engagement and Generation T. Lowe's Companies, Inc.

"I have known Robert Rodriguez for close to two decades. In that time I have seen him become the premier expert on how to elevate ERG performance in corporate America."

—Isaias Zamarripa,
Global Diversity and Inclusion, Bristol Myers Squibb

"I have seen the power that ERGs have to meaningfully energize people, strengthen connections, and promote transformation. Dr. Rodriguez knows better than anyone in business how to curate, organize and resource these individual organizational assets. This book is both a must-have and a gift to anyone trying to achieve ERG excellence."

—Shannon Trilli Kempner,
Vice President, Corporate Responsibility and Diversity & Inclusion, Catalent Pharma Solutions

"ERGs are one of the first elements of a diversity & inclusion strategy most organizations kick-off on their journey towards greater equity. Robert's knowledge, research, and actionable recommendations ensures that ERGs are set up for success and benefit both the employees and also the organization. Don't try to launch ERGs without the expertise and guidance provided by Dr. Rodriguez in this book."

—Bo Young Lee,
Chief Diversity & Inclusion Officer, Uber Technologies, Inc.

"Dr. Robert Rodriguez has been a trusted advisor, and major asset, to us in the area of ERGs by providing Facebook with critical guidance, strategic insights and creative solutions. His deep expertise and credibility are why he is such a sought-after diversity leader and influencer."

—Barbara Furlow-Smiles,
Global Diversity & Inclusion Engagement Leader, Facebook, Inc.

"Robert has been a steadfast advisor to State Street's Employee Networks for many years. We owe a lot of our growth to adopting his 4C approach and strategy. This book is a must-read for those ERG leaders and diversity practitioners looking to turbocharge their networks."

—Paul Francisco,
Chief Diversity Officer, State Street Corporation

"Dr. Rodriguez's 4C ERG strategic framework is a best-in-class model for moving towards ERG excellence. The 4C Model creates employee resource groups that are business-focused and impactful to business results."

—Jessica Rice,
Global Head of Diversity, Equity, and Inclusion, Under Armour

EMPLOYEE RESOURCE GROUP EXCELLENCE

ROBERT RODRIGUEZ, PhD

EMPLOYEE RESOURCE GROUP EXCELLENCE

GROW **HIGH PERFORMING ERGs** TO ENHANCE DIVERSITY, EQUALITY, BELONGING, AND BUSINESS IMPACT

WILEY

Published by John Wiley & Sons, Inc., Hoboken, New Jersey.
Published simultaneously in Canada.

Library of Congress Cataloging-in-Publication Data is Available:

ISBN 9781119813743 (Hardback)
ISBN 9781119813767 (ePDF)
ISBN 9781119813750 (ePub)

Cover design: Wiley

SKY10029627_090721

To Mom and Dad: Thanks for all the sacrifices you made to help give me more opportunities and a better life. This book extends your legacy of always giving back to the community. Little did you know that your decision to move our family to Minnesota would lead to the start of my lifelong connection with employee resource groups. All my love.

To Bailey and Benjamin: I can have no greater ambition in life than to be the best father I can be to you both. You are yet too young to have launched your professional careers, but if you should be fortunate enough to work for a company someday that has employee resources groups, I hope that you will join an ERG and that your ERG experience will be as rewarding as mine has been. I love you both.

To Sofia: You'll always be the love of my life. Thanks for your unwavering support, not only during the writing of this book, but in sharing me as my ERG consulting commitments often requires extensive travel away from our home. Who knew that it would be an ERG event that would bring us together? Te Amo.

To companies: Thanks for all you do to support employee resource groups. May this book help you create the conditions that will nurture ERG excellence.

To ERG members and leaders: This book is dedicated to you, due to your willingness to give back and commit your time and energy above and beyond your day jobs to help run and maintain your employee resource groups. This book is my gift to you for all that ERGs have provided me during my lifetime. I will be forever grateful.

CONTENTS

INTRODUCTION: THE MILLI VANILLI SYNDROME

My Personal Connection to Employee Resource Groups

The city of Matamoros in Mexico seems like an odd place to point to as the origination point for this book that eventually was destined to be titled *Employee Resource Group Excellence*. Matamoros is a city in the northeastern Mexican state of Tamaulipas. It is located on the southern bank of the Rio Grande, directly across the border from Brownsville, Texas.

Matamoros is the birthplace of my father, German. My father is the oldest of eight children, all of whom were born and raised in or near Matamoros. When my father reached the age where he could work, he would go across the border to work in Brownsville, Texas. It is in Brownsville that my father eventually met my mother, Janie. Janie is Mexican American, but she is a United States citizen, born in Texas. After a short courtship, German and Janie married and settled in the city of Lubbock, located in the panhandle region of Texas.

Lubbock is the city where I was born in 1969. My memories of Lubbock are rather vague, as we lived there only until I turned four years old. Our family, along with my aunts, uncles, and cousins, used to travel to the Midwest every year as migrant workers. We would go to cities like Traverse City, Michigan, to work the cherry fields and Wahpeton, North Dakota, to help with the sugar beet harvest. We eventually settled on the west side of St. Paul, Minnesota, which is where I grew up and spent my youth during the decades of the 1970s and 1980s.

This upbringing is what led me to eventually join employee resource groups. You see, Minnesota is a great place to live, and was a great place for a child to grow up. However, during my formative years as a child, there was not a large Hispanic population in the Twin Cities, which is what Minneapolis and St. Paul combined are called. Other than my extended Hispanic family that settled in Minnesota with us, there were not many other Latinos. Even today in 2021, the percentage of Hispanics living in Minnesota is still only approximately 5 percent. It was definitely much less back in the 1970s.

My parents, who were well intentioned, encouraged me to connect with the local Anglo kids in the neighborhood. Soon you would find me on the hockey rinks in the winter and baseball fields in the summer. Friends and neighborhood kids to hang out with were not too hard to find, but almost none were Hispanic like me. Additionally, my parents encouraged me to assimilate within the predominantly white community in which we lived. For example, instead of learning to dance Mexican cumbias or rancheras, I learned American dances and the polka – there were lots of polka bands at weddings and parties in Minnesota, I soon realized.

Assimilating and downplaying my Hispanic heritage served me well in high school and even in college. While I was not ashamed of my Hispanic heritage, I wasn't leaning into it nor celebrating it. It simply was not a big part of my identity. My cousins who had remained in Texas and decided not to move to Minnesota were more fluent in Spanish, more knowledgeable about their heritage, and wore their Latino identity on their sleeve. I guess it is easier to celebrate your Hispanic heritage when you are surrounded by a large number of Hispanics.

Anyhow, after finding academic success in high school and in college, it eventually came time to join corporate America and start my professional career. My first two jobs were with large corporations, Target Stores and 3M Company. My jobs with both of these companies were based in Minnesota, so I naturally followed the same routine as when I was in school. That is, I identified as Hispanic, didn't deny it but also did not celebrate it either nor manifest it to a great degree.

Milli Vanilli

Back in the late 1980s and early 1990s, the pop duo group known as Milli Vanilli was hugely popular and successful. The group had several hit songs, including "Girl You Know It's True," "Blame It on the Rain," and "Baby Don't Forget My Number," each reaching the number 1 ranking on the Billboard Hot 100. I even admit to liking the group and their songs.

With their good looks, catchy songs, and appealing videos, Milli Vanilli went on to win a Grammy for Best New Artist in 1990. The two members of Milli Vanilli, Fab Morvan and Rob Pilatus, were adored by fans and loved by the music industry. Unfortunately, it was eventually discovered that while Rob and Fab appeared in the Milli Vanilli music videos and performed at the concerts, it was not their voices that were recorded on the album. Once word got out that other artists supplied the vocals on the album, Milli Vanilli was dropped by their record label, their various awards were taken away, and they were shunned by everyone and ultimately became famous for being fakes and inauthentic.

While the Milli Vanilli scandal played out, my career was progressing nicely. I was performing well in my job and was gaining respect at work, making many new friends and professional colleagues. So well in fact that I was deemed early in my career as someone who had high potential for accelerated career advancement. At the time that I was working at 3M, any young professional who was rated as having high potential had to participate in the company's leadership assessment program. The program consisted of taking a personality indicator (I took the Myers-Briggs Type Indicator), having one-on-one interviews with leadership development experts, completing an inbox work simulation exercise, and participating in a 360-degree feedback review session where a group of my peers and reporting staff comment on my performance and what I am like to work with.

Overall, my assessment results were strong, and I continued to get promoted about every 18 months or so – I was on the fast track. However, there was one bit of feedback from my 360-degree review that I will never forget. One of my peers indicated that I came across as inauthentic because it appeared to them that I was downplaying or hiding certain aspects of myself so as not to appear different, and that I was disassociating from one of the dimensions of my identity. This peer knew that I was Hispanic, but since I wasn't really embracing my Hispanic heritage at work, to him I came across as being inauthentic: "He sort of reminds me of Milli Vanilli because he makes me think he is faking something, and I'm not sure I can trust someone who is faking."

Ouch. This comment stung. Still stings to this day. I had never felt like I was being a phony at work. I never claimed to be someone I was not. But apparently, to this one other person, that is exactly how I was coming across. The leadership development expert who was assigned to review my results told me that because my results were so strong, I shouldn't worry too much about this one single comment. She reminded me that every bit of feedback is a gift if it helps a person improve or raise their awareness. I was happy with the results of the assessment, but the Milli Vanilli comment stuck with me for many years. Little did I know, however, that this would initiate my eventual employee resource group involvement.

After several short job assignments in various small towns in the Midwest in which 3M had manufacturing facilities, eventually my career required a relocation to Chicago. Of course, I was excited that I was going to a big metropolitan area. Little did I know at the time that this move would be the start of my journey to become more connected with my Hispanic heritage, and it is what led me to seek out and join employee resource groups. This happened in part because several things changed upon arriving in Chicago and connecting more closely with my Hispanic heritage.

First, the Hispanic community was much larger in Chicago than it was in Minnesota. I went from Hispanics being less than 5 percent of the population in Minnesota to being close to 30 percent of the population in Chicago. Being surrounded by a much larger Hispanic community made it much easier to connect with other Hispanics besides my family. Second, the Latino community in Chicago was much more diverse. In Minnesota, the Latinos in my circle were predominantly of Mexican descent. But in Chicago, the Hispanics were not just Mexican but also Puerto Rican, Dominican, Cuban, Guatemalan, Colombian, Venezuelan, Peruvian, and so on. This exposed me to a much broader perspective of what it meant to be Latino. The third big difference was that many of these Hispanics were professionals with advanced degrees, and almost all held professional roles such as doctors, attorneys, entrepreneurs, engineers, marketing professionals, academics, and politicians. Not only did I know and meet very few Hispanics when I lived in Minnesota, but only a small percentage of them were degreed professionals working in corporate America like myself.

The biggest difference, however, was that many of the Hispanics I met were unapologetically proud of their heritage. They embraced it. They didn't hesitate to speak Spanish, eat at Hispanic restaurants, play Latin music, talk about what was happening in Latin America, or partake in Hispanic customs. In short, they were leaning into their Hispanic heritage, and being Latino was a big part of how they identified themselves. Not only did they celebrate being Hispanic, but they also wanted others to celebrate it with them. Many of the Latinos I initially met upon moving to Chicago were connected to nonprofit professional associations such as the Hispanic Alliance for Career

Enhancement or the Hispanic National Bar Association, which means they were also active in the Latino community.

My career path had now taken me to work at Amoco Corporation, the oil and gas company based in Chicago at that time. In connecting with this large, professional, diverse, and proud Hispanic community, I was searching for a group at my work to support my growing desire to lean into my Hispanic heritage. Enter the Amoco Hispanic Network (AHN), the Hispanic employee resource group at Amoco at the time. Many of my fellow Latinos at Amoco were members of AHN and they encouraged me to check it out. At first, I wasn't sure what the focus or purpose of the group was, but the concept of professional Latinos purposefully meeting while at work intrigued me and piqued my interest.

My connection with AHN was immediate. I instantly became involved and joined as an official member. I loved working with other Hispanic professionals and enjoyed a sense of freedom I hadn't felt before about being Hispanic at work. I still recall my first event – a Cinco de Mayo event held in the company auditorium in 1997. The focus of the event was to educate non-Latinos that Cinco de Mayo was not Mexican Independence Day. The members of AHN were tired of constantly having to explain to non-Hispanics the significance of this day. The feeling of helping others gain better awareness and understanding about my Hispanic heritage was satisfying. Not only did I want to learn more about my culture and have a stronger connection with my heritage, but the Amoco Hispanic Network taught me that we could educate others as well. This was my very first experience with employee resource groups, and I was hooked from the very beginning.

After working at Amoco for a few years, the company merged with British Petroleum in 1998. At the time, it was the largest industrial merger in US history. Eventually, my stint at Amoco ended and I went to work at RR Donnelley & Sons, the printing company also based in Chicago. Having had a positive experience with the Amoco Hispanic Network, I inquired if there was a Hispanic employee resource group at RR Donnelley; unfortunately, there was not. There was, however, a multicultural employee resource group called the Professionals of Color ERG. I joined and eventually became the chair of the group in 2001.

Like my experience with the Amoco Hispanic Network, my involvement and leadership of the ERG at RR Donnelley was quite rewarding. I soon found myself developing a strategy for the group, allocating resources, ensuring member engagement, and finding ways that I and others could bring our full selves to work, as they say. The chair role was also raising my visibility and exposure within the company, because many of my ERG duties involved meeting with executives and leaders within RR Donnelley whom I likely would not have met through the duties of my day job alone. Overall, I was having a blast and performing well as a leader of this employee resource group.

Ironically enough, after my ERG experiences at Amoco and RR Donnelley, I never again worked at a company that had employee resource groups. Yet the foundation had been set. I was thankful that the ERGs had raised my visibility, my capability, and my promotability. But the single biggest benefit I received from being involved in employee resource groups is that they helped me find my voice. The ERGs allowed me to gain confidence in being my true, authentic self. The combination of moving to Chicago and then joining employee resource groups helped me to understand that my Hispanic heritage was an asset and a source of strength. That leaning into my ethnic identity not only made me feel more authentic, but I also came across as more authentic to others. Never again would anyone say I reminded them of that damn Milli Vanilli group!

And thus, the foundation was set. I decided then and there that I would always support employee resource groups and talk about the many benefits they provide. If employee resource groups could have the same impact on others that they had on me, then I felt an obligation to help them grow and prosper within organizations. After earning my doctorate and eventually launching my own consulting firm, Dr. Robert Rodriguez Advisors (DRR Advisors) in 2012, it was clear that I was going to dedicate a significant amount of energy and consulting engagements to helping organizations create the conditions that will nurture ERG success and be a resource for ERGs and their leaders.

It is hard to put into words the influence that employee resource groups have had on my life. Not only did ERGs help with my career advancement, but they also helped me to become my true authentic self. My experience in an employee resource group provided the safe environment that I needed to embrace my Latino sense of identity. ERGs opened my eyes to seeing my world in a whole new way.
My ERG experience allowed me to see life in brilliant color.

I often describe my experience of joining an employee resource group as being similar to the movie *The Wizard of Oz*. For those of you who have seen the movie, you'll recall that at the beginning, Dorothy is in Kansas and the movie is in black and white. Soon the twister (tornado) comes and scoops up Dorothy and whisks her away. Then there is that glorious scene when Dorothy awakens and opens the door of her house that has landed in Oz, and suddenly her world is shown in brilliant color. To me, when I joined an employee resource group, it was as if my world transformed to color. I could see all the richness and beauty – not only in my own Hispanic heritage, but in the promise of diversity and inclusion itself.

Employee resource groups have also provided me a comfortable living. Consulting to organizations on their ERG initiatives is quite lucrative, and my ERG consulting fees have afforded me and my family a life of comfort. And of course, ERGs have allowed me to meet amazing people all over the world. People who, like me, believe in the power of employee resource groups. People whom I now call my friends and who live in all four corners of this Earth. Ultimately, I am confident that this book will trigger a new wave of energy, research, and appreciation of employee resource groups. I believe that we have only just begun to uncover all the hidden value that exists within ERGs. There are still too many people who haven't experienced the joy and impact an employee resource group could provide them.

And so here we are, from my humble beginnings as the son of Mexican American migrant workers raised in Minnesota, to my struggles with my Hispanic identity and being perceived as inauthentic, to eventually joining and becoming a leader of employee resource groups. All this led me to where I am today, which is arguably being considered one of the nation's top experts on employee resource groups. This book seeks to capture all my experience working with employee resource groups, as well as the findings from studying and researching ERGs. This knowledge will be supplemented throughout the book with real-life examples of employee resource groups that convey excellence. Add to this my trained academics eye for noticing underlying theoretical foundations and the nation's largest collection of ERG data analytics obtained through my 4C ERG Assessment™, and this book is sure to provide unique insights and strategies aimed at elevating ERG impact and performance.

In considering the arc of this book, in Part 1 we'll first explore the current state of employee resource groups before talking about common ERG derailers before celebrating ERG leaders. From there, the book transitions into Part 2, which includes a deep dive on the 4C Model and the 4C ERG Assessment, two of my inventions and things I consider to be my gift back to the employee resource group community. We will explore each of the 4C (career, community, culture, commerce) pillars in great detail and outline how they contribute to employee resource group excellence. The book culminates with Part 3, which focuses on ERG solutions and strategies and ends with what I call the ERG Excellence Manifesto.

My goal is that this book will trigger a new way of thinking about ERGs. I look forward to providing a roadmap that leads all employee resource groups toward excellence.

1 Beyond Food, Flag, and Fun

The Current State of Employee Resource Groups

The aspirations for this book are not meek, nor are they muted. The purpose of this book is to help employee resource groups (ERGs) achieve excellence. Every company that has approached me to help with their ERGs wants to know how to get them to perform at their best and with distinction. This book intends to inform these efforts.

In today's polarized world, employee resource groups are now more necessary than ever. The work of ERGs is too important, and the need is too great, for them not to perform at their best. My experience with employee resource groups goes back 30 years to my first jobs in corporate America back in the early 1990s. Ever since, my relationship with employee resource groups has evolved and matured and resulted in having a much more textured understanding of, and appreciation for, all the great things employee resource groups provide.

This personal journey with employee resource group includes being an ERG member, an ERG leader, running ERG consortiums, conducting research on ERGs, establishing contests to identify "best-in-class" ERGs, helping companies launch ERGs, serving as a judge to determine the top ERGs in the country, writing ERG white papers, and helping ERG to pivot on their strategy and so on. It is without any hesitation that when it comes to employee resource groups, I have seen the good, the bad, and the ugly. This extensive experience uniquely positions me to write this book – see Table 1.1.

Companies ranging from Amazon to Zillow have all asked me to help with their ERGs. Working with large companies, like Walmart, and small companies, like Zebra Technologies, has given me a unique perspective of ERGs that is not matched by many others. Seeing these groups operate in every industry allows me to take a step back to notice ERG trends, observe best practices, identify key derailers, and hear the discourse associated with these groups. This puts me in a very privileged position. My academic training, including a doctorate in organization development, helps in the analysis of how employee resource groups operate within their larger organizational systems.

This book intends to share these lessons learned and insights. In doing so, the goal is to further help organizations create the conditions that nurture ERG success. For ERG leaders and ERG members, this book will help you create ERGs that have a holistic impact on your members, the company, and the broader community.

The Very Heart of Diversity and Inclusion Efforts

I'm sure that most readers of this book work at organizations that have a diversity and inclusion (D&I) mission statement. Some are short but effective: "To create, nurture and sustain a global, inclusive culture, where differences drive innovative solutions to meet the needs of our customers and employees." Others are a bit more elaborate: "As both a global and local business, diversity and inclusion are at the heart of our values and is an important part of our company's success. For us, creating a diverse and inclusive workplace is not only the right thing to do – it is a strategic business priority that fosters greater creativity, innovation and connection to the communities we serve."

Table 1.1 Dr. Robert Rodriguez Partial List of ERG Consulting Clients (2017–2021)

Abbott	CBRE	Intel	NBCUniversal
AbbVie	Chevron	JetBlue Airlines	Nielsen
Adobe Systems	Cisco	Johnson &	Nike
Akamai	Comcast	Johnson	Northern
Technologies	Cox Enterprises	KMPG	Trust
Alcon	Cracker Barrel	KraftHeinz	Northwestern
Allstate	Diageo	Levi Strauss & Co.	Mutual
Alto Pharmacy	Discover Card	Liberty Mutual	Oppenheimer
Altria	E.J. Gallo Wine	LinkedIn	Funds
Amgen	Electronic Arts	Lockheed Martin	Pacific Gas &
Anheuser-Busch	Eli Lilly	Lowe's	Electric
Aon Hewitt	Ericsson	Manpower Group	Prudential
Associated Bank	Facebook	Mass General	Insurance
Astellas Pharma	FannieMae	Brigham	Raytheon
Asurion	FiatChrysler	McDonald's	Technologies
Baxter Healthcare	General Electric	Corporation	Sanofi
Biogen	Gilead Sciences	McKesson	SC Johnson
BCBS -	GlaxoSmith Kline	3M	Sony
Massachusetts	Google	Medline	Stanley Black &
Blue Shield of	Gusto	Medtronic	Decker
California	Hallmark Cards	Merck	State Street
BMO Harris	Harley Davidson	MetLife	Corporation
Bank	Harvard	Micron	SurveyMonkey
Boeing	University	Technology	The TJX
British Petroleum	Health Care	Microsoft	Companies
Brunswick	Service Corp.	Mondeléz	Uber
BSE Global	Henkel	National	Under Armour
C.H. Robinson	Corporation	Basketball	Verizon
CapitalOne	Herman Millar	Association	VMware
Catalent	Hyatt Hotels	National Credit	Walgreens
Pharma	Ingredion	Union Association	Zillow

Dr. Robert Rodriguez
Partial List of ERG Consulting Clients (2017–2021)

But regardless of whether the diversity and inclusion mission statements are short or long, the message is the same. Everyone benefits from having a diverse employee population who feel included in the organization. This synopsis of common mission statements puts employees at the very core of diversity, equity, and inclusion efforts. So, in my opinion, employee resource groups must be at the very heart of any effort to improve the workplace from a diversity and inclusion perspective.

You see, every company says, "Employees are our most important asset," yet few rarely act as if this is true. Embracing and nurturing groups that are run by employees (a company's most important asset) to drive diversity and inclusion (a company's strategic priority) to promote equity (a company value) just goes to show why employee resource groups are critical. Given the important role ERGs play, it is no wonder they are prolific within organizations. Yet, it is still astonishing that ERGs are still mostly treated as a simple tool in the D&I toolbox, as opposed to being the very essence and manifestation of diversity and inclusion itself.

Why is the pursuit of ERG excellence so important? First consider the current environment of today's organizations. Companies are having to adapt to a workplace that has an increasingly diverse and global employee population. This diverse workforce demands inclusive work environments. Employee resource groups help to create these inclusive environments.

More diversity in the workplace calls for leaders who can effectively manage this diversity. Gone are the days when a manager could treat every employee the same way. Today's diverse workforce requires managers to be more inclusive. It requires them to know what motivates each employee and the unique strategies that allow them to get the most out of everyone. Diversity requires managers to use a variety of strategies, approaches, and methods to maximize employee performance. A one-size-fits-all strategy to managing large groups of employees is not effective. Thus, the demand for more inclusive leaders has risen. Employee resource groups help an organization create the more inclusive leaders they need.

Even though organizations have increased diversity overall, employees from historically underrepresented communities are still lacking in most senior leadership teams. Organizations need to do better in grooming executives that come from a more diverse pool of candidates. With their focus on career advancement, ERGs help to create a more representative talent pipeline.

Not only have workplaces become more diverse, so has our society in general. The population growth in the United States is being driven by multicultural communities. The growing size of these minority populations means that their purchasing power is increasing. Thus, companies must cater to a consumer base that is less homogeneous. Multicultural marketing departments have grown in size as organizations look to penetrate previously overlooked market segments. If companies are to leverage diverse markets as a catalyst for economic growth, they need cultural intelligence. Employee resource groups provide this cultural intelligence.

Increasingly, employees want to work for employers that are socially conscious. They want employers who are good corporate citizens in the communities in which they operate. To accomplish this, organizations need employees who are closely connected to their communities. They need employees who want to give back to their neighborhoods, districts, and regions. Organizations also want employees who are involved in local nonprofits because this helps to build bridges with community organizations. Employee resource groups help companies establish stronger relationships in the community.

For these reasons, and many more, organizations need their ERGs to deliver on their goals. We need our ERGs to perform at their peak. And we need organizations to expand their value proposition to all their stakeholders. We are not asking for perfection from our employee resource groups. Perfection is not the goal. The goal is a desire to achieve excellence. The dictionary definition of excellence is "to surpass"; it is "the quality of being outstanding or extremely good." When ERGs strive for excellence, they are always looking at where they are and how they can get a little bit better. And since we will be discussing the concept of ERG excellence throughout the book, I'm going to define it here at the very beginning of our journey.

As we continue along this book, we will periodically pause to reflect how this definition of ERG excellence came to exist and how it manifests itself in our organizations.

> ERG excellence is a commitment to a data-driven approach, resulting in an inclusively holistic value proposition in which employees drive accelerated career advancement, improved cultural competency, enhanced community relations, and greater company success.

Employee Resource Group Basics

Prior to launching on our journey to ERG excellence, let's take a quick glance at these groups. These groups go by many names, including affinity networks, power of difference communities (PODs), employee networks, and diversity councils. The most common names used to refer to these groups are employee resource groups or business resource groups (BRGs). This book will reference the groups mostly as ERGs and occasionally as BRGs.

So, what are employee resource groups? ERGs are inclusive communities in which the members tend to share some common characteristics. ERGs usually focus on traditionally underrepresented groups within organizations and are typically based on gender (women ERGs), ethnicity (Hispanic ERGs), race (Black/African American ERGs), sexual orientation (LGBTQ ERGs), physical capabilities (disability ERGs), shared experience (military veterans ERGs), age (young professional ERGs), or some other common characteristic (parents ERGs). They typically are formed by employees after receiving the approval by the company to establish an employee resource group.

ERGs are quite prevalent in organizations, with approximately 90 percent of the Fortune 500 companies having employee resource groups. Organizations usually have between six to eight employee resource groups with the occasional company having a dozen or more separate ERGs globally. For example, AT&T, the global media, and communications company, has 37 separate employee groups and networks across their enterprise.

When companies do have ERGs, the minimum penetration rate any organization ought to achieve is 10 percent. This means that at least 10 percent of the organization's employees are members of at least one of their employee resource groups. ERGs can exist with a penetration rate less than 10 percent, but it is difficult for these ERGs to thrive in such situations because they lack the sufficient critical mass of the employee population. A gold standard would be a penetration rate of approximately 20 percent. Best in class numbers that I have seen are a penetration rate of about 40 percent. Just imagine, almost half of an organization's employees identifying as a member of an employee resource group.

The obvious question then becomes, what constitutes being an ERG "member"? Sadly, that is a question that does not have a universally accepted answer. Some companies simply count the number of employees who wish to be placed on an ERG email distribution list as members. Other organizations require employees to formally acknowledge and disclose their membership in an employee resource group through self-identification. And yet some organizations require a certain level of participation in ERG initiatives before they are counted as a member. This leads to the question of who is considered to be an "active" member. Penetration rates simply use the membership definition chosen by each organization.

My diversity consulting firm, DRR Advisors, conducted a study in 2020 on the average annual investment allocated by companies towards employee resource groups. The study included an analysis of 175 organizations with ERGs and found that the average annual investment allocated to each employee resource group was approximately $8,800 per year for every 100 members. This means that if an employee resource group has 100 members, on average it received an annual budget of $8,800 per year from the company. If an ERG has 200 members, on average it receives an annual budget of $17,600 per year and so on. This represents a 22 percent increase in ERGs budgets since 2011, when ERGs received on average $7,200 per every 100 members, according to a study by the global equality, diversity, and inclusion practice at Mercer. This equates to an average budget increase for employee resource groups of approximately 2.44 percent per year from 2011 to 2020. Personally, I'm aware of one company where the annual budget allocated to just one of their employee resource groups (their women's ERG) is over $1 million per year. A significant investment indeed.

But before we celebrate ERG budget investments, interestingly enough, however, the average annual inflation rate in the United States, according to the US Federal Reserve Bank from 2011 to 2020, is approximately 2.4–2.6 percent. This means that while ERG budgets have increased, these budgets are simply helping ERGs keep up with the inflation rate and thus do not demonstrate any significant progress. So, while organizations have been lauding the importance of their employee resource groups, they have not increased their investment in them over the last decade. ERG excellence hopes to change that.

The allocation of budgets varies from organization to organization. Some companies allocate ERG budgets based on membership, with ERGs that have larger membership receiving more funds than ERGs with fewer members. Other organizations allocate funds based on a business plan. An ERG puts together a business plan for the year indicating its planned initiatives, including an estimation of how much they will need to successfully execute these initiatives. The company then determines how much of their requested budget outlined in their plan they can give an employee resource group. Some companies provide every ERG the same budget amount, regardless of the size of the group. And some companies, albeit only a few, charge employees a fee to become a member of an ERG, and these fees help to fund the employee resource group. I am aware of several organizations where employees pay an annual fee of $25 to be a member of an employee resource group. Interesting approach indeed.

Once launched, employee resource groups tend to go through a natural evolution over time. Initially, the ERG tends to focus on the more social aspects of the group with a concentration on building community via events promoting networking and establishing connections with people of similar background or interest. Over time, ERGs expand their focus to include career development initiatives for their members and an increased emphasis on external community outreach. Eventually, they launch initiatives aimed at having a greater alignment with business priorities and organizational goals.

And yet, despite this increased impact, many ERGs are in the midst of a major inflection point fraught with uncertainty about what direction to take to remain relevant. We have to ask ourselves why some employee resource groups have prospered, while others have floundered. How do external trends impact this internal groups? What unexpected challenges await today's ERGs? And what principles must

ERGs live by in order to effectively deal with the changing landscape of contemporary global business?

While some managers marginalize and trivialize ERG contributions, other leaders fully appreciate the value ERGs can provide as they feel a sense of responsibility to addressing pressing societal and business issues if they are to build a global inclusive and respectful workplace and develop a global workforce competent to work effectively with an even more diverse set of colleagues and clients.

Seeing Global ERGs as Simply Overseas Extensions of US Groups

Some organizations are worried that a typical response to diversity and inclusion will make them fall short of their goals. That is, seeing global ERGs as simply overseas extensions of US diversity initiatives. As ERGs have gone global, companies have found the most success with groups dedicated to women, LGBT employees, and those with disabilities. Young professionals have also lent themselves to a global ERG approach as they face some shared challenges within organizations around the world. These kinds of networks continue to proliferate quite naturally.

Some efforts flow from a master global strategy while others surface quite organically in the absence of a global strategy, in response to the universal experience of societal pressures, taboos, and even legal restrictions that force people to hide who they truly are in order to have a chance at success.

Going global opens up additional unexpected dimensions that have universal appeal. For instance, one professional services firm has a Global Athlete's Network, which aims to connect people "who are involved in and passionate about the top echelons of sport," including high-level coaches, elite athletes, and those involved in organizing major sporting events or training camps.

The objectives of this group are instructive in the unique take they have on the role of sports in networking within the organization. The following goal and objectives are listed on the company's intranet:

> The goal of the network is to gather insights and ideas so that we can offer a unique perspective to clients. To realize this goal, we have established a set of objectives that address the firm's client and talent agendas:
>
> - Establish a global network of people with a common interest in elite sport, who can share knowledge and experience ranging from training tips to managing a balanced lifestyle.
> - Provide a real example of where our talent is "Always one step ahead" that illustrates our company's commitment to high performance, flexibility, and choice.
> - Apply high performance and coaching expertise to our business.
> - Support the development of a center of excellence in delivering major sporting events that can be leveraged throughout the global organization through sporting event knowledge.

So far, the network covers 28 countries and 24 Olympic sports.

Addressing the issue of race and ethnicity around the globe is a greater challenge, however. How does a Latino employee group go global when Latinos in Latin America are the majority and find the whole concept of ERGs foreign? How does an African American group establish a global presence when many Africans look at Black ERGs and see them as more American than African? How do companies address race and ethnicity in places like Peru, China, and France, where people prefer to talk about things other than race (even when they indeed have racial and ethnic societal tensions)?

Accelerating the evolution of ERGs so that they address both domestic and global diversity and inclusion issues will be explored throughout the book. Pushing ERGs to have a holistic value proposition as they strive toward excellence is the main focus of this book.

ERG Trends

Before launching into tips and strategies on how to achieve ERG excellence, it is important to determine the environment that ERGs are operating in today. These trends have been forming for the last 36–48 months but were accelerated in 2020 due to the global Covid-19 virus pandemic. Employee resource groups have had to learn to pivot and adjust in a world where people are coping with a pandemic, struggling with economic uncertainty, dealing with racial inequality, and adjusting to working from home.

Yet even with all these headwinds, employee resource groups are still prevailing. Their resiliency is impressive. Such resiliency is why employee resource groups have existed in corporate America since the early 1970s. In 1970, Joseph Wilson, the former CEO of Xerox, and Xerox's Black employees launched the National Black Employees Caucus. This caucus is considered by most to be the nation's first official employee resource group. The ability for employee resource groups to evolve ever since is what keeps them relevant and what allows them to persist and endure, even in the most difficult workplace environments. With a better understanding of ERG basics and insights about the environments ERGs are operating in, let's explore the trends that are shaping ERGs today and informing how they will operate tomorrow.

Alignment with Talent Management

Organizations are leveraging employee resource groups not only to help them groom their next generation of company leaders but also to make ERGs a destination for existing leaders. ERGs help companies identify an even larger, more diverse, pool of employees who have the potential to become leaders. But now, companies are also encouraging those deemed high performers, and as having high potential, to consider becoming more actively involved with ERGs.

Employee resource groups have always provided leadership development opportunities, especially for ERG leaders. Imagine being an employee who is an individual contributor in their current role with limited opportunities to demonstrate their leadership capabilities. Now put that same employee as the leader of an employee resource group, and suddenly the employee is developing a strategy, leading a team, managing a budget, establishing new relationships with co-workers, and raising their visibility and exposure to corporate executives. Access to such leadership experiences is often a reason many employees join an employee resource group.

However, companies do not want to create a scenario where the ERGs are helping to groom leaders only to have those leaders leave the employee resource group. Organizations need leadership continuity in order for these groups to have sustainable long-term success. And this has resulted in the greater alignment of ERGs with talent management.

Alignment with talent management initiatives often involves ensuring that strong performers are in the leadership roles of the ERGs. If the employee resource group does not have a strong leader, companies are now starting to appoint someone to the role of ERG leader who is more capable. The person appointed is increasingly someone who is already deemed a high performer or someone with tremendous potential.

The reasons for the need to appoint strong performers into ERG leadership roles are twofold. First, companies realize that employee resource groups tend to be only as strong as their leader. Second, the demand for strong ERG leaders often exceeds the supply. And this has led to greater ERG alignment with talent management. This will be explored further in Chapter 11.

Underutilized Business Assets

There has been much fanfare about turning "employee resource groups" into "business resource groups." The thinking goes that ERGs cannot just be the "food, flag, and fun folks" who are primarily focused on the social aspects of employee resource groups. Organizations want ERGs to have a broader value proposition. The goal is not to eliminate the social aspects of employee resource groups because we still want them to celebrate over food, waive their diversity flag, and hold events that are indeed fun. But we need to encourage ERGs to also add value in a more holistic way. This broader value proposition is something that I have been advocating for many years as a component of the definition of ERG excellence.

Yet, in my experience, ERGs are not the ones to blame if they do not have a more direct impact on helping an organization meet their goals. In working with thousands of employee resource groups for the past several decades, these ERGs want to have a direct impact on the organization. They are often more than ready, willing, and able to support business initiatives. The real problem exists with the organization itself. Surprisingly, organizations are woefully inadequate at leveraging their ERGs for business impact. This results in employee resource groups being an underutilized business asset still today. We will explore this phenomenon, and how to overcome it, in Chapter 8.

Metrics-that-Matter

In my experience, ERGs have long struggled with articulating the value they provide back to their members and to the organization as a whole. Any measures of success an employee resource group touts typically involves a listing of their activities and membership size. ERGs are quick to tell you how many members they have, across how many locations, and how many events they held in the past year. While these numbers help, they do not adequately convey to others how successful the ERGs are. The lack of metrics is one reason that middle managers often do not give ERGs the credibility and respect that they deserve. What is needed by employee resource groups is a more sophisticated measurement strategy, a strategy that not only highlights the ERG's activities, but also the impact of those activities.

ERGs need to have metrics that help them tell their story and inform others why they exist. I call these "ERG metrics-that-matter." Without such metrics, employee resource groups are unable to track their progress or compare themselves to benchmark standards. ERGs are not solely to blame for this lack of metrics. Organizations are often reluctant to share data and information that ERGs can use to establish such metrics. Also, not having metrics makes it impossible to have a scorecard or dashboard where an ERG can easily share their results. If an ERG does have a scorecard or dashboard, it tends to usually be a qualitative analysis of their activity as opposed to a quantitative report on their impact. The lack of a measurement strategy is how many ERGs are operating today and we will explore this further in Chapter 10.

Succession Planning

One reason for greater alignment between ERGs and talent management is that ERGs do not typically engage in succession planning. The purpose of succession planning is to make sure an ERG always has the right leaders in place should a leadership change happen quickly or unexpectedly. The lack of succession planning is one reason that some employee resource groups struggle to sustain early success.

The Covid-19 pandemic had a tremendous impact on ERG leadership. Some existing ERG leaders left their roles because they had to concentrate solely on their day job. Some left because they were downsized or quit their jobs to focus on their family. And some left their role as an ERG leader because they simply could not run an employee resource group under the challenging Covid-19 work environment. Those who were able to remain in their ERG leadership role often indicated that the search for the next ERG leader should begin. These individuals burned out due to all the heavy lifting they had to do to run an employee resource group effectively during the dynamic and unprecedented period that began in 2020.

All this sudden and concentrated leadership change at the top of many ERGs has exposed insufficient pipelines of new potential ERG leaders. Not enough ERG members have been groomed to assume leadership roles of an employee resource group. Additionally, companies have not adequately made ERG leadership roles highly desired, resulting in fewer employees wanting these roles. This succession planning crisis, and all its implications, will be analyzed in Chapter 5.

Skeptical Middle Management

One thing that has not changed much in the past 10–15 years is that middle managers at organizations still are mostly skeptical about the value of employee resource groups. These middle managers struggle to see the benefits that ERGs provide. Some are still convinced that ERGs are divisive as opposed to being entities that promote unity and inclusion.

I once spoke to a focus group consisting of managers at one company who saw a lack of engagement by middle management as a key obstacle for their employee resource groups. It was difficult to blame some middle managers for not being more supportive of ERGs because they simply didn't know what these groups were about. Some were not aware they even existed or lacked clarity as to what ERGs do. Given such lack of awareness about ERGs, it was easy to see why there were not more supported.

Other middle managers were more transparent and shared their concerns about employees spending too much time on ERG activities and not enough time on their regular job. These managers shared their reality of having too few resources to meet challenging goals and that they need their employees focused on their work. And still others conveyed the impracticality of allowing their employees to attend ERG meetings or events when it required their employees, who were mostly hourly, to be at their desks answering calls or on the production line putting out product.

Regardless of the reason, ERGs need more active engagement from middle management. They need managers to support employees who wish to participate in employee resource group activities. Better yet, ERGs need more middle managers themselves to join employee resource groups. But in order for this to happen, both employee resource groups and middle managers have to do their part.

Employee resource groups need to do a better job of defining their value proposition (including metrics-that-matter) to middle management. Employee resource groups must convey how and why their activities are relevant to middle managers. Conversely, middle management should be more proactive in finding out what ERGs are all about and why these groups are prevalent across corporate America and what employees get out of their involvement. However, until both stakeholder groups accomplish this, the lack of middle management support is a reality that ERGs must contend with for the foreseeable future. The strategies highlighted throughout this book will hopefully convince more middle managers of their importance in endorsing and advocating for ERGs. The lack of middle manager support will be analyzed further in Chapter 2.

Narrowing ERG Ambitions

Employee resource groups are struggling to deal with two goals that appear to be mutually exclusive. On the one hand, employee resource groups have been expanding their value proposition beyond just social activities. Employee resource groups now have robust career advancement initiatives; they strive to elevate the cultural competency within an organization; they support community outreach and as mentioned previously; and they desire to make a larger business impact.

But employee resource groups' budget resources have been depleted due to the changing work landscape that began in 2020. ERGs membership numbers took a dip as overall employment levels dropped. Some companies reduced the budget dollars they had previously allocated to their ERGs, citing reduced budget cuts across the organization as the reason. And with employees now working from home, many previously planned ERG events and gatherings simply were not feasible. The result is employee resource groups with big ambitions being confronted with the reality of a new workplace. The bold plans and activities that ERGs had at the beginning of 2020 have been reduced. Employee resource groups have had to pivot in an environment that now places greater emphasis on prioritization. "Underpromise and overdeliver" is the new mantra being embraced by employee resource groups under this new reality.

Some employee resource groups are handling this transition effectively. They eliminated events that did not align with the overall mission of their ERG. There is increased collaboration amongst the employee resource groups as they partner to do events jointly in an effort to reduce the redundancy that results when ERGs operate in silos. Employee resource group leaders have become better skilled at saying "no" or "not now" when ideas for future activities are given by ERG members. And ERG leaders have improved at delegation, resulting in a broader array of members contributing to doing ERG work. Yet the question remains that when things go back to normal, if they ever will return to how things were before, will ERGs continue with the less-is-more mentality? Will they be successful in having a broad value proposition while being more selective in their pursuits?

I believe the answer is yes, but only time will tell how employee resource groups will operate after the effects of the pandemic have passed.

ERG Leader Development

For many, many years, it was surprising to see organizations ask much of their employee resource group leaders but offer little to help them be successful. ERG leaders are still often left on their own to figure out how to elevate member engagement, develop an ERG strategy, and manage a group that is made up of employee volunteers with no direct reporting relationship. ERG leaders have been asked to articulate their impact on the organization without being given access to data to measure such impact. Companies want metrics from their employee resource groups but offer no training to the leaders on how to establish appropriate metrics. I could go on and on, but you get my point; much is asked of ERG leaders when often not much is given to them in the form of organizational and development support.

Fortunately, many organizations have seen the error of their ways. But to be clear, we are not talking about professional development workshops that ERGs offer their members. We are talking about professional development that organizations offer to the leaders of their ERGs with the goal of making them more effective.

There is tremendous growth in the number of companies holding regular internal ERG summits. These summits usually bring together the leaders of ERGs to hear from corporate executives, learn about diversity and inclusion goals, network with other ERG leaders, hold panels with ERG leaders at other organizations, and so on. These summits usually require a significant investment by an organization. Some companies that do not hold their own ERG summits will send their ERG leaders to external organizations that organize ERG conferences focused on professional development.

In some cases, an employee resource group does not hold a summit per se, but invests in professional development workshops for their ERG leaders. Occasionally, existing internal professional development content is delivered exclusively to employee resource group leaders, especially if such development content might not be available to the employee.

For example, the home improvement retail organization Lowe's Companies, Inc., based in Mooresville, North Carolina, conducted a session for its business resource group leaders on how to use a new internal assessment tool that helped identify employee work style and communication preferences. BRG leadership team members were given the assessment so that each could assess their own effectiveness. The business resource groups were shown how they could generate a report that outlined the communication and work style preferences of their BRG leadership team, all in an effort to help the business resource groups operate more effectively together.

And on occasion, external speakers are selected to provide development to the leaders of employee resource groups. This is how many companies engage with me. I've worked with numerous companies – such as Capital One, Under Armour, Catalent Pharma, The TJX Companies, and Uber, to name a few – where I have established an ERG Leadership Academy that consists of providing regular professional development workshops for their ERG leaders.

Whether it be internal ERG summits, external ERG conferences, or access to professional development workshops, the purpose is the same: to develop the skills and capabilities of leaders so that they can be even more effective at guiding their employee resource groups. This trend is long overdue, and it is gratifying to see so many organizations embrace the idea of ERG leader professional development.

Let's remember why we need employee resource excellence. Excellence is about continuously looking to improve, striving to do the best you can, and looking for ways to be a little bit better than yesterday. When employee resource groups strive for excellence, they are forced to focus on the things they already are doing well.

ERG excellence is a daily, never-ending journey. ERG excellence requires that the majority of ERG focus is on the things that are working really well and on the next thing they can do, which is often within their reach. Striving to do better is incredibly motivating and inspiring because all employee resource groups have an innate desire to do better. ERGs want to excel.

2 The Seven Deadly Sins

Derailers That Prevent ERG Excellence

In our journey toward ERG excellence, we must address potential derailers – behaviors demonstrated by an employee resource group that get in the way of their effectiveness, progress, and ability to make an impact. A derailer is different from a weakness. Every employee resource group has weaknesses. A derailer is a weakness that requires improvement and therefore must be addressed.

When a train accidently comes off its tracks, it is called a derailment. The world *derailer* is thus a metaphor for something coming off its intended course. The use of the word *derailment* is appropriate for this book because these behaviors pose an obstruction of a process by diverting employee resource groups away from their intended destination of excellence. By studying common ERG derailers, we can hopefully avoid them or at least try to minimize them so if they do appear, they only temporarily deflect employee resource groups from their pursuit of excellence.

When derailers begin to appear, they limit or undermine ERG effectiveness. Derailers not only hurt performance; if not addressed quickly, they cause employees to not want to join an ERG. In my experience, some derailers create more problems than others with regards to hindering performance and the pursuit of excellence. But if employee resource groups become skilled at spotting potential derailers, they can learn to avoid them or to work through them as they pursue optimum performance levels.

The work of employee resource groups is too important, and the need to have effective ERGs is too great, for us not to try to prevent derailers. Too many individuals have given up their free time and exerted a great amount of personal energy to create employee resource groups that truly make an impact. Because of this, we cannot allow derailers to prevent employee resource groups from meeting their objectives.

In 2018, I was involved in a consulting engagement with Verizon Corporation. Part of the engagement was to assess their employee resource groups. We distributed my 4C ERG Assessment™ online questionnaire that was completed by over 2,200 of their ERG members. The results of the 4C ERG assessment were overwhelmingly positive and demonstrated that the employee resource groups at Verizon were performing well and had many areas of strength that could be leveraged to sustain their success.

A portion of the online questionnaire did ask the ERG members to review a list of common ERG derailers (see Table 2.1) and to indicate if they felt their employee resource group was beginning to experience or exhibit any of these behaviors. To their benefit, only a few derailers were selected as potentially posing a threat to the employee resource groups at Verizon. One derailer that many ERG members felt was potentially threatening their impact was a concern over a lack of succession planning and leadership continuity within the employee resource groups. With this insight, I worked with members of the diversity and inclusion team at Verizon to help establish a more sophisticated approach in identifying future leaders of their employee resource group and to ramp up their ERG leader

Table 2.1 Most Common ERG Derailers

A - Ineffective in partnering with other ERGs and often operates in a silo.	B - Fails to nurture and provide needed development to ERG leaders.	C - Takes an "us versus them" mentality when interacting with other ERGs, HR, or diversity and inclusion.	D - Not able to get the entire leadership team on the same agenda.
E - Unable to embrace a strategy that is more aligned with talent and business outcomes.	F - Fails to look at succession planning and leadership continuity issues.	G - Fails to communicate effectively between the national ERG chapter and the chapters at field locations.	H - ERG consistently seen as demonstrating inflexibility, defensiveness, and impatience.
I - Fails to align ERG leadership roles with talent management to groom future leaders.	J - Inability to effectively address "Peers managing Peers" issues.	K - Fails to understand how ERG fits into "big picture" and that the ERGs are an extension of the diversity and inclusion strategy.	L - Does not evolve as the needs of the organization change. Wish to remain focused on a very narrow value proposition.
M - Failure to prepare adequately to ensure ERGs are capable of making a business impact.	N - Focuses on events vs. integrating ERG into talent management, business practices, and community outreach.	O - Lacks ability to accurately gauge an organization's pace of change and advocates work plan that moves too quickly.	P - Frequent disregard of company protocols related to communication, funding, or external-facing activities.

selection and succession planning process. The Verizon organization, and their ERGs members, realized that a lack of leadership continuity could significantly hurt the overall impact of their employee resource groups. The proactive approach to specifically ask ERG members about potential derailers is an excellent example of a proactive step a company can take to mitigate the risk that derailers present.

The goal of this chapter is to help employee resource groups avoid blind spots by highlighting the most common derailers. To be clear, we are going to focus on derailers specific to employee resource groups. Since ERGs are by definition a team, they are prone to experience derailers that might impact any sort of workplace team. For example, I've seen highly cohesive ERGs fall into the trap of *group think*. They failed to critique their own thinking and could not see that a lack of different perspectives was holding them back. Another common team derailer that I've seen emerge within an employee resource groups is failing to learn from experience. Some ERGs tend to repeat the same mistakes over and over again without questioning the assumptions they are making.

Since almost all ERGs tend to have a single leader, co-leader, or a leadership team, they are also prone to common leadership derailers. I've seen power struggles for leadership and control within employee resource groups. This creates tension between the leadership of an ERG and its membership around the way power and authority are exercised within the employee resource group. Another common leadership derailer I've seen is when the leader is a perfectionist. Such leaders fail to recognize when something is good enough, and they tend to become obsessive or uncompromising.

Seven Deadly ERG Derailers

It goes without saying that employee resource groups should take steps to avoid typical team and leadership derailers. But our focus here is to identify the most common derailers specific to employee resource groups. ERGs should pay careful attention to these derailers and, like Verizon, periodically check to see if any are beginning to appear. Without knowing what these ERG derailers are, however, it becomes more difficult to avoid them. So, as we strive for excellence, let's explore these ERGs derailers by first helping to define the behavior and then by providing a specific example of derailer.

1. Big Picture Derailer

This occurs when an employee resource group fails to understand how they fit into the "big picture" of the organization. This is a derailer because the ERGs do not recognize that they need to be in alignment with a company's overall purpose and that they are an extension of the diversity and inclusion strategy. Employee resource groups that tend to fall into this trap focus almost exclusively on their membership. There is nothing wrong with this per se, but when it comes at the expense of supporting the overall purpose and goals of the organization, it can limit the overall effectiveness of an employee resource group.

For example, I recall working with one global manufacturing company that had been involved in several mergers and acquisitions over a five-year period. The company was now ready to streamline operations across their 11 disparate operating companies. One approach the company took was to revamp their supplier diversity program. This was done to mitigate risk and exposure, ensure supply chain resilience, and localize control of the bill of materials. The goal was to leverage supplier diversity improvements to increase earnings-per-share for the organization.

The D&I team approached several of their employee resource groups to become more aware of the company's supplier diversity initiative and to seek ways that they could support these efforts. Some ERGs helped spread the word to their membership about upcoming training sessions they could attend related to supplier diversity. Other employee resource groups allowed members of the supplier diversity department speak at some of their ERG member meetings to raise awareness and answer questions.

However, of the company's eight employee resource groups, three of their ERGs indicated they did not wish to support supplier diversity efforts. They did not see how supporting supplier diversity efforts was part of their ERG mission. They refused to allocate time on their agenda for supplier diversity personnel to speak, nor did they announce upcoming supplier diversity meetings to their membership. Worse still, they did not respond to requests for help in identifying new potential suppliers that were majority owned by women or underrepresented minorities. These three employee resource groups were failing to see the importance of aligning their efforts with company goals. They failed to see that the benefits of an improved supplier diversity program helped the company, and thus helped their members. Their lack of support for the supplier diversity initiative reduced their credibility and respect among middle managers at the company. This proved to be detrimental to the ERGs who lost membership because of lack of manager support and thus proved to be a derailer for them. This is why it is important for employee resource groups to understand how they fit into the big picture related to the organization's strategy.

Contrast the approach taken by this company to the approach taken by the ERGs at Catalent, Inc. Catalent is a global leader supporting the delivery and manufacturing of pharmaceutical products. In February 2021, I was asked to participate in their ERG Summit, which lasted three days. After serving as the keynote speaker for the summit, I stayed to listen to several of the speakers on the agenda. What impressed me was that a significant part of the agenda had been allocated to the leader of Catalent's Diverse Supplier Program. This speaker shared critical details about the program and outlined the program benefits on a global scale. Most importantly, the speaker outlined how the employee resource groups could help. By learning more about Catalent's Diverse Supplier Program, the ERGs were demonstrating that they understood the big picture.

2. Pace of Change Derailer

This derailer appears when the employee resource group lacks the ability to accurately gauge an organization's pace of change and advocates for a work plan that moves too quickly, is too aggressive, or at times not fast enough. These ERGs tend to lose sight that there are other priorities in the organization in addition to what is on the ERG agenda. Yes, it is true that we want ERGs to be agents of change, but employee resource groups need to understand that each company implements change at different speeds. Some are quicker and readily embrace change. Others tend to be slow and methodical when it comes to organization change. The key is for ERGs to understand the pace of change within their organization and try to follow the same tempo.

In 2020, Twitter announced that they would begin compensating members of its business resource group leadership teams for their extra work. In 2021, LinkedIn followed Twitter's example and decided to pay their ERG leaders $10,000 per year for their ERG leadership role. This was formal recognition of the importance that both Twitter and LinkedIn placed on their employee resource groups. The ERGs at another smaller organization in the transportation industry heard about Twitter's and LinkedIn's compensation decision and they insisted that their company do the same. While company leadership was not necessarily opposed to the idea, they did want the ERGs to mature a bit more as the employee resource groups had only been formed a few years prior. Several of their ERGs were not yet fully established and several had only a few short-term wins and accomplishments to highlight. Plus, the company wanted to do some benchmarking with peer companies to see if they too were considering compensating their ERG leaders.

The ERG leaders at the company took this response by the company as a failure to recognize the value of their work. They felt that asking them to expand their value proposition and to wait while the company did some benchmarking was simply a stall technique. One ERG leader was so disappointed that the company wasn't following Twitter's and LinkedIn's lead immediately that he actually stepped down from his role as president of one of the ERGs, citing that if the company didn't value his contributions by compensating him, he did not wish to continue leading an ERG. The company may well decide to compensate their ERG leaders via additional pay or some other type of recognition. But if it does, it will do so when the company believes it is best prepared to do so. But the fact that the ERG leaders were demanding that the change be implemented immediately demonstrated that they were not in step with the pace of change within their organization.

At times, a company may ask an ERG to help accelerate change. For example, when protests were occurring in the United States connected to the death of George Floyd, many companies leaned on their employee resource groups to help them better understand the issue of systemic racism and the importance of demonstrating allyship towards Black, Indigenous, and People of Color (BIPOC) communities. For their signature event for Hispanic Heritage Month in 2020, the Latino ERG at Cox Enterprises held a workshop focused on allyship and intersectionality. The goal was to accelerate the development of their Latino ERG to become even more effective allies to the Black community. They realized that the moment called for a higher sense of urgency of Black allyship within the Cox Enterprises. This is a demonstration of an employee resource group that is in step with the pace of change not only with their company, but with the broader collective sentiment of the moment.

3. Self-Serving Derailer

Employee resource groups that demonstrate self-serving tendencies often press for their priorities and are indifferent to the needs and interests of other stakeholders. ERGs that fail to identify and partner with key internal sponsors often convey their willingness to go it alone, often with devastating results. ERGs that fall into this trap do not connect the dots or recognize the interdependence between ERGs and other departments. It is not uncommon for self-serving ERGs to alienate colleagues and/or run roughshod over other ERGs' agendas. Another characteristic of self-serving ERGs is their failure to consistently develop and maintain constructive, and supportive, internal relationships with others.

In 2019, I facilitated a workshop on the importance of ERG collaboration for a commercial real estate services company based in Dallas, Texas. I was asked to speak on this topic by the chief diversity officer of the company because he felt that the ERGs were operating as silos and were not partnering sufficiently in his opinion. The result was a lot of redundancy in their activities and a failure to understand what each of the other ERGs were doing. In this particular company, the problem was being driven by their Women's ERG, whose executive sponsor was the company CEO. Whenever the Women's ERG wanted something or felt that a rule didn't apply to them, they went to the CEO. The CEO, thinking he was being helpful, often granted the wish of the Women's ERG without understanding the broader consequences. The result was a Women's ERG that often didn't follow the rules, failed to collaborate with others, and didn't seen too interested in how the other ERGs were doing. As a result of having the CEO as their sponsor, the Women's ERG had a much larger budget than all of the other ERGs and often got other special privileges and treatment, which tended to exasperate not only the other employee resource groups but also the diversity and inclusion department.

During my workshop on collaboration, I noticed that all the employee resource groups had representatives at the session with the exception of one, the Women's ERG. When the diversity and inclusion team approached the Women's ERG as to why they were not in attendance at the workshop, they informed them that they decided to hold their own Women's ERG leadership team meeting as opposed to participating in the workshop. The Women's ERG felt they didn't need to collaborate with the other ERGs because their employee resource group had strong membership, held well-attended events, and had high engagement. What the Women's ERG was failing to realize is that they were being resented by the other employee resource groups because they weren't following the same rules. An even bigger worry was that the leaders of the Women's ERG were not grasping the importance of interdependence and relationship building, all of which could prove detrimental to their individual careers and perceived leadership readiness in the long run.

4. Rule-Breaking Derailer

Similar to the self-serving derailer, ERGs that tend to frequently disregard company protocols often succumb to the rule-breaking derailer. These ERGs often do whatever they feel like when it comes to things like communication, funding, or external-facing activities. Worse still, these ERGs tend to take an "us versus them" mentality when interacting with other ERGs, human resources, or diversity and inclusion. This often results in an ERG having a relationship with others that can best be described as combative or confrontational. Not only is this not healthy, but it tends to diminish the reputation of all employee resource groups, even those that are following the rules and are operating in a more collaborative manner.

Sometimes this behavior can manifest itself in smaller ways. I once had a client engagement with a company that had trouble reigning in one of their ERGs when it came to the subject of sending out email messages to their membership. The organization had policies in place regarding mass-distribution emails pertaining to how often they could be sent, to whom they could be sent, the content of such email messaging, etc. Several of the ERGs simply ignored these protocols because they felt the policies were too restrictive and prevented them from communicating effectively to their membership.

Soon, however, employees began to opt out of receiving ERG-related emails because they felt they were getting too many of them or that they simply weren't clear or effective in communicating their desired intent. When the employee resource groups were approached to comply with company protocol, several did so but only for a short while, and soon they were again sending out a large number of email messages to their membership. In essence, what these ERGs were saying is that company protocol did not apply to them, and they demonstrated a combative attitude with the communication department. Eventually, one of the ERGs sent out an email that did not follow company protocol regarding hiding the names on the distribution list. The email was sent by the Disability ERG at the company, and by not hiding the names of the distribution list, several members felt their identities had been shared with others without their consent. This proved especially problematic for members who had hidden disabilities or desired not to disclose to others that they had a disability.

Rule breaking does occur within ERGs, but most often it is inadvertent and usually not repeated. Protocols and policies are established by a company for a variety of reasons. Most are intended to protect the organization and to protect the employees. When employee resource groups convey a willingness to disregard such protocols, it positions them as an outlier. We can appreciate that sometimes employee resource groups want to push the envelope. But an ERG that consistently tries to work outside of the boundaries of an organization is very rare and is setting itself up for failure. When the employee resource group needs help, others may not be willing to provide support due to their past rule-breaking behavior. Such behavior also tends to be divisive, which goes against the very core of why ERGs exist. An "us versus them" mentality also conveys a sense of superiority by some and a sense of inferiority of others. Again, this is not what ERGs are meant to convey. ERGs that continue to demonstrate such behavior may be doing so because they believe it is in the best interest of their membership but in actuality, the employee resource group is harming the team mentality with the other ERGs. They tend to promote unnecessary conflict and competition and ultimately harm inter-ERG cooperation in the long run.

5. Peers-Managing-Peers Derailer

We understand that employee resource groups and its members tend to be volunteers and that ERG leaders have no real authority over their members. But occasionally employee resource groups have an inability to effectively address "peers managing peers" issues. Typically, an ERG leader is selected from the existing ERG membership. This means that any new leader was recently a peer to his or her fellow ERG members. Also, it's not too uncommon to have the new ERG chair who is an individual contributor with several of the ERG members holding manager- or director-level positions. This can cause awkwardness if the ERG leader is not comfortable giving directions to someone who has a higher job title. An ERG leader might experience difficulty establishing their credibility without acting as if their ERG leadership role has gone to their head. Some ERG leaders might find it challenging to now lead their former ERG member peers because it requires others to recalibrate their relationship with the ERG leader. The result could be an ERG leader who is too timid and afraid to take the leadership reigns assertively and with conviction.

If not handled well, ERGs can soon demonstrate other derailer-type behaviors such as forming cliques, excessive gossip, turf battles, and infighting. Another common result of the inability for peers to manage peers is that the ERG soon begins to have difficulty dealing with conflict or differences of opinions. They tend to avoid such issues and this results in failure to keep ERG issues on the table until they are resolved. When conflict is avoided and issues are brushed under the rug, the issues fester and become bigger problems.

In 2016, a client asked me to serve as a coach to the new leader of their Veterans ERG. This new leader had only left active-duty service in the Navy two years prior with the rank of ensign. The new leader was a bit concerned because several members within his ERG had been members for a considerable amount of time, and several had held higher ranks in the military, including a few that had left the military with the rank of captain or lieutenant. In addition to being outranked by a few of his ERG members, he faced the challenge that several others held higher-level job titles than he held. He was excited to assume the ERG leadership position but didn't want to come across as if he was saying, "I'm in charge now."

I advised him to do a few things that I often tell new ERG leaders to do. First, do not forget about his new peers, the leaders of the other ERGs at the company. So, he set off to get to know his fellow ERG leader peers so that he could build mutual credibility and respect with them. Second, I advised him to connect with the other ERG member who had expressed interest in the ERG leadership role. He made it clear to this ERG member that he was important to the success of the employee resource group and that he would advocate for his development and potentially groom him to be his successor.

Next, we established an approach where he could identify a few small decisions he could make fairly quickly, including a new schedule for ERG member meetings and a new set of expectations related to ERG communications. This allowed him to demonstrate his ERG leadership without stepping on toes or damaging relationships. He liked the idea of treading lightly at first and deferring bigger decisions until he'd been in the role longer, which gave him time to gather additional information from the broader ERG membership. Finally, we outlined a strategy for him to establish his authority. He met with the employee resource group as a group as well as held a few individual meetings with the ERG members who had higher ranking when they were in the military. He shared with them his vision for the employee resource group and his approach to leadership. In these meetings, the new ERG leader was advised to do more listening than talking. This showed that he was in charge of the ERG but also conveyed that he was there to support the broader ERG. I recently checked in on him and he informed me that he had served a successful three-year term as the chair of the Veterans ERG and that no issues ever materialized by those who had outranked him or by those who held higher roles. He thus avoided the peer managing peer derailer.

6. Decision-Making Derailer

Every ERG must make decisions related to their strategy, implementing the strategy, allocating resources, establishing priorities, and so on. But in my experience, a huge derailer is when an ERG is not able to act in a decisive manner. It would be easy to place the blame on the ERG leader for this, but in my experience, it is when the ERG collectively has difficulty making decisions that leads to the most significant problems.

Because employee resource groups are not entities where individuals have formal authority over others, they tend to decentralize their major decisions to a leadership team and at times to the entire membership. In my experience, employee resource groups tend to make decisions by consensus. But ERGs often find that a decision-making derailer can be linked to a talent taken to an extreme. There are situations where the leader of the team must make the decision for the ERG. This can occur when a rapid decision needs to be made or when the ERG leader has all the necessary information needed to make the correct decision. But even in some of these scenarios, ERG leaders at times still find themselves asking the team to provide input on a decision when it might not be necessary. This is likely to occur when the ERG leader lacks confidence and is overly concerned with avoiding the risk of making a mistake that can be unilaterally blamed on them. In this scenario, the derailer is having an ERG leader who is indecisive.

Another common scenario of the decision-making derailer is when the ERG leader(s) convey to the membership that the members will be allowed to make a certain decision on something important to the ERG. The membership, believing that the leaders will support whatever they decide, then inform the leaders of their decision. If the ERG leaders do not agree with the decision made by the ERG membership and override their decision with something different, that is when the derailment tends to occur.

For example, one of my recent engagements involved helping to bring together the employee resource groups of two companies that recently merged. In this case, I was working with their Hispanic ERG specifically. The two new co-chairs of the Hispanic ERG indicated that they would allow the membership to choose the name of the employee resource group, and several names were provided for consideration. The ERG would go with the name that received the most votes from the ERG membership. The name that received the most votes from the membership was Latinx & Allies ERG. However, the two co-chairs did not like the term *Latinx* and were very surprised that it had received the most votes from the membership. They informed the group that *Latinx* was not a real word, that it was a polarizing word in the community, and that having Latinx in the name of the ERG would cause confusion. They decided to ignore the wishes of the membership and went with a name that did not include the term *Latinx*. The derailer that happened here is that the leaders had informed the membership that they had the authority to select the name of the group. It turns out that this was not the case, as ultimately the co-chairs overruled the choice made by their members. By outlining a decision-making process and then not sticking to it, the dynamics of the ERG were immediately off to a terrible start. The leaders had violated the trust of the members, and their leadership ability lost credibility.

7. Poor-Leadership Derailer

This derailer is the one that occurs most often and can have the biggest negative impact on an employee resource group. On numerous occasions I've seen this derailer significantly limit the impact and progress of an ERG. Yet this derailer is the most difficult one to avoid because it can manifest itself in a variety of ways. In some cases, poor leadership is displayed because the ERG leader(s) lack focus. They are easily distracted, shift from one priority to another, and ultimately fail to get anything done. When an ERG leader is not able to focus the efforts of their ERG, it is almost impossible for the group to have an impact.

Other times, the poor leadership derailer occurs when the ERG leader(s) are selfish, and their own personal agenda supersedes that of the employee resource group. This can occur when leaders select an initiative that has limited impact for the ERG but does allow the leaders to meet often with key executives, thus only elevating the visibility and exposure of the ERG leaders. When ERG leaders are selfish, it is not too uncommon for them to come across as aloof, distant, or unapproachable. An ERG leader who is selfish also tends to be closed-minded, in that they tend to avoid initiatives that don't place them in a good light and are often unwilling to consider other viewpoints.

Some ERG leaders cause derailments because they are micromanagers. They become overly controlling and do not empower others with freedom or latitude to do their best work for the employee resource group. Micromanagers also cause derailment because they create significantly more stressful ERG environments. This may cause ERG members, who are volunteers after all, to become demotivated, disengaged, or quit being in the employee resource group altogether. Micromanagers also tend to lose their tempers quickly and lack patience when things are not done their way. This, too, tends to irritate the other ERG leaders.

Most poor ERG leaders are lacking a gut feeling for the gestalt of their employee resource groups. That is why their actions and behaviors tend to quickly derail an ERG. However, the poor leadership derailer can be mitigated via careful selection of who has the privilege leading employee resource groups, providing them with sufficient leadership training and having them monitored closely by D&I and their executive sponsors.

Advice that I give to just about every client is to have their employee resource groups look at the most common derailers listed in Table 2.1. Each of these derailers is preceded by a letter in the alphabet. Then, taking an approach outlined by Verizon earlier in this chapter, have the ERG membership anonymously indicate if they feel that any of these derailers are starting to appear within their ERG by simply listing the letter that corresponds to a specific derailer. Once all the responses have been provided, an organization can quickly identify if any derailers are listed frequently as existing within their employee resource groups so that steps can be taken to correct. This is a proactive step towards derailment mitigation.

Sometimes, a derailer exists that is not the fault of the ERG. One, in particular, is the middle management derailer. If middle managers within an organization do not hold the ERG in high regard or provide support of employee resource groups hesitantly, it could significantly hurt the group's probability of success. Most of the time, this lack of support by middle managers is because they do not have a clear understanding of how ERGs are relevant to them. That is why some ERGs go to great lengths to convey to middle managers that ERG initiatives ultimately help them reach their goals, albeit sometimes in an indirect way.

The ERGs at one financial regulatory institution periodically hold an ERG Fair in their company cafeteria, at which a table is set up with brochures that describe what employee resource groups are, what employee resource groups currently exist, the benefits to members if they join, a summary of past ERG initiatives, and outline steps to join. The table is usually staffed with current ERG members who can answer questions from interested employees.

But one thing in particular that the ERGs do at this particular organization is to hand out a brochure that interested employees can give to their immediate supervisor or manager. This brochure is specifically created for middle managers and explicitly outlines the benefits to them, the middle manager, when their employees join an ERG. In doing so, the employee resource groups are conveying to middle management why ERGs are relevant to them.

This particular brochure highlights nine ways they benefit when employees join an ERG:

1. *Hands-on leadership experience*. Employees gain valuable leadership experience managing teams and overseeing ERG budgets.
2. *Presentation skills*. ERG members frequently present to company executives, which builds confidence and presentation ability.
3. *Developing others*. ERG leaders develop other employees, and they bring these coaching skills back to their home departments.
4. *Collaboration*. ERG members expand their network and enhance their collaboration skills with employees in other departments or other job levels.
5. *Strategy awareness*. ERG members gain greater insight into corporate strategy due to ERG alignment with organizational goals.

6. *Business acumen.* Some ERG leaders manage the budget for the employee resource group, thus enhancing their business acumen and ability to determine ROI.
7. *Community involvement.* By volunteering, ERG members enhance the organization's reputation and brand in the community.
8. *Diversity champion.* ERG members learn how to champion diversity and can promote diversity and inclusion in their home departments.
9. *Employee engagement.* Company surveys show that ERG members have a higher level of engagement as well as a higher retention rate than non-ERG members.

Besides the brochure targeted at middle managers, other initiatives created by ERGs to mitigate the risk of a middle manager derailer include establishing a middle manager advisory council for ERGs or emails from executive sponsors to managers when an employee does an outstanding job within the ERG.

Excellent ERGs are brilliant at the basics. They don't let tools substitute for strategic thinking. Intellect does not overpower wisdom. Analysis does not impede a bias for ERG action. Almost all ERG derailers can be avoided through intentionality and monitoring. If employee resource groups follow basic management and high-performing team techniques, derailers won't prevent them from striving for excellence.

3 Movers and Shakers

Nurturing the Success of ERG Leaders

Not enough can be said about the leaders of employee resource groups. Here are individuals who, despite working their full-time jobs, are still willing to raise their hand and commit to leading an ERG to help an organization reach their diversity and inclusion goals. It takes someone truly special to make this commitment, and their willingness to contribute and give back should always been applauded. ERG excellence cannot be achieved without leaders who are passionate, highly motivated, well respected, and strategic. In just about every ERG engagement that I embark on, I give a special shout-out to the leaders of these groups. ERG leaders should receive all of our deepest respect not just for what they do, but for who they are.

Having been an ERG leader myself at one point in my career, I can also attest that at times the job can be daunting, intimidating, frustrating, and sometimes thankless. Many ERG leaders have shared how they have put in long hours, given up a lot of their free time, and sacrificed things they love in order to excel in their role. Yet even when ERG leaders do all this, there are still some who like to complain, are quick to critique or fail to participate or to attend events that ERG leaders have worked very hard to put together simply because they forgot.

It is in these situations that it is always a good idea to remind ERG leaders that their work is too important, and that the need for diversity and inclusion is too great, for them to become discouraged and give up. Every organization has to do all that it can to support ERG leaders, train them, and create the conditions that nurture their success. And most importantly, it is critical to remind ERG leaders that their efforts make a difference and that they are likely having a larger impact on their members and on the organization than they realize. For the efforts of ERG leaders are likely resulting in more employees feeling like they belong at their organization. Their efforts are helping to create future leadership teams that have an even more diverse profile. ERG leaders create initiatives where a greater percentage of the workforce feels like they can be their true authentic selves. Because of ERG leaders, our workplaces have more allies who not only proclaim their allyship but do things to help those in need feel their allyship.

It is clear we owe a huge amount of gratitude to ERG leaders. This appreciation is sure to be well received by ERG leaders who often do not seek recognition, but nonetheless take pride in seeing their efforts acknowledged. But as organizations, we need to do more. Too often, organizations simply do not do enough to assist their ERG leaders. They outline the requirements and expectations of ERG leaders but then fail to provide them the training and resources critical to their accomplishing these goals. So, this chapter outlines what must be done by organizations to set up their ERG leaders for success.

Outline ERG Leadership Benefits

Almost all ERG leaders take on these governance roles because they want to give back and to help shape the success of D&I efforts. But it is prudent to remind these leaders of the personal benefits they can obtain from these roles. Not that they need to hear these benefits for them to take on the leadership role, but as a motivator to keep moving forward when things can get a bit challenging or discouraging.

First, leaders are charged with establishing the strategic plan for the ERG. This is a significant responsibility and an incredibly important skill to develop, particularly for those whose day job may not allow them to do much strategic planning. Thus, ERG leaders develop the ability to continuously scan the organization to identify value creation opportunities and synergistic collaborations across departments as they pull together a strategic plan. The ERG strategic planning process also forces the leader to analyze and, if necessary, reframe root causes for what is contributing to the gap between the ERGs current state and desired future state. Ultimately, ERG leaders gain the ability to insightfully identify root causes to entrenched ERG problems and develop clear, simple, and targeted approaches that explain the circumstances and pave the path toward a solution.

Second, ERG leaders gain valuable leadership experience. By leading an ERG, they become the person responsible for the execution of the strategic plan. They chart the course and develop the initiatives and approach to achieve the goals for the group. ERG leaders ultimately learn to inspire others to increase their effectiveness as inclusive leaders and demonstrate sincere support for the success of others. Effective ERG leaders also gain the ability to persuade others to pursue a particular action – despite natural or inherent resistance. The ability to understand what motivates others and design an approach to leverage those motivators is a key leadership capability gained by ERG leaders. During their term as ERG leaders, they eventually demonstrate measured confidence and authenticity through congruence of action and word. For those who are individual contributors and limited leadership experience, serving as an ERG leader provides the chance to develop this skill set.

Managing a budget is also a key responsibility for ERG leaders. Being able to effectively allocate resources and then track the use of company-provided funds provides another wonderful learning opportunity. Since financial resources allocated to employee resource groups are at times limited, the ERG leader thus must learn how to prioritize funds so that they provide the maximum benefit to the group. Over time, the ERG leader becomes quite skilled at building a compelling business case for yearly and multiyear ERG budgets that demonstrate solid understanding of financial and economic drivers to achieve results. Almost all ERG leaders also gain the ability to grasp the discourse of business – why ERGs exist, its underlying principles, its enablers, and threats.

From my perspective, the biggest benefit of leading an employee resource group is gaining the visibility and exposure that comes with the role. ERG leaders often have to meet with their executive sponsor and other senior-level leaders. When ERG leaders perform well, this ability to demonstrate their capabilities to an executive audience is invaluable. When executives are impressed by the skills and capabilities of an ERG leader, it is more likely that the executive will advocate for their career advancement and further help to accelerate their upward mobility. I'm aware of dozens of examples shared with me by former ERG leaders, who indicated their promotional velocity accelerated after performing well in the ERG leadership role. The benefits of being an ERG leader are pictured in Figure 3.1.

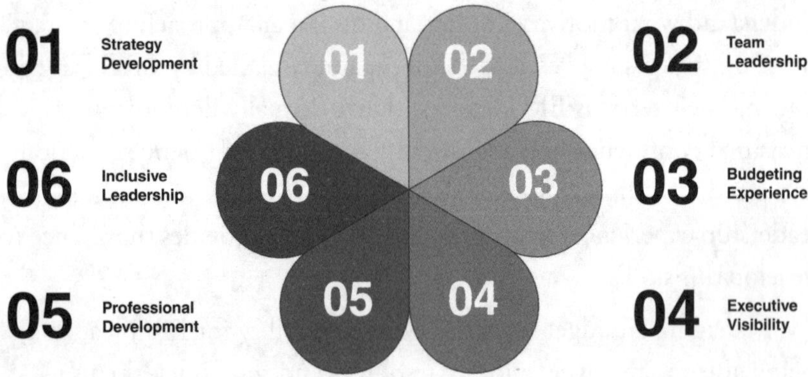

Figure 3.1 ERG leader benefits.

ERG excellence dictates that companies invest in the continual professional development of their ERG leaders. Organizations simply cannot set high expectations of their ERG leaders and then not provide them with developmental opportunities to gain the skills and capabilities necessary to run an employee resource group. In my experience, there is a high level of correlation between the skill development provided to ERG leaders and the overall performance of the employee resource groups. Thus, ERG excellence demands an intentional strategy toward ERG leader development. While this may sound commonsensical, it is still not commonplace enough.

Individual Contributor as ERG Leader

Organizations should particularly support the ERG leader who is an individual contributor in their day job. That is to say that their role within the organization does not include any supervisory or managerial responsibility because they do not have direct reports. These individuals likely aspire to the ERG leadership role because of the developmental experience it will provide them. Sure, it is true that they will gain valuable leadership capability through their ERG leader role, but organizations must help them succeed. As an individual contributor, they likely do not possess many of the skills required of an ERG leader. Organizations that hope that these individuals simply learn "while on the job" are taking a huge risk. A better approach is to help individual contributors who assume the ERG leadership role gain proficiency in three key areas: their work skills, how they apply their time, and what they need to value as an ERG leader. Let's explore each in more detail.

Work Skills

From a skills perspective, an individual contributor tends to rely on skills focused on their technical proficiency, being a strong team player, the capability of building relationships, and ultimately following the rules, processes, and procedures set up by their supervisor. All of these will definitely help them as the ERG leader and a high level of capability in these areas is likely what led to them being selected to be the leader of the employee resource group.

But as the leader of the employee resource group, they will need to apply skills that they might not possess. For one, their ERG leadership role will now require them to plan the work of others, something that might not be required of them as an individual contributor. Some of their fellow ERG colleagues might also require coaching as they try to accomplish their ERG tasks. Again, coaching others might not be required of them in their day jobs. Employees who are in individual contributor roles also rarely have to define expectations for others, nor is it likely that they have experience in selecting or appointing people to complete various tasks. These both are also areas in which they will need a certain level of skill proficiency if they want to perform well as an ERG leader.

Time

Besides having to apply skills that they have not yet mastered, individual contributors now have to allocate their time differently as ERG leaders. For employees who do not have direct management responsibility, most of their time is allocated toward applying daily discipline to getting their work done on time. But in their role as an ERG leader, the employee will now have to allocate time toward things like creating the ERG strategic plan, making themselves available to their fellow members, setting priorities for various ERG committees, and finding the time to connect with the leaders of the other ERGs, the D&I department, and with their executive sponsor. Many new ERG leaders without previous management responsibility struggle with the increased demands on their time.

Values

An ERG leader also needs to adjust to new values regarding their work. For the employee who is an individual contributor, their work standards are mostly focused on doing their job through personal proficiency, producing high-quality work, and other tenets such as punctuality, content, and reliability. All of these are necessary and honorable, but their success as an ERG leader will require them to take on additional responsibilities. They now will have to place greater focus on getting results through others and not just on their own performance. They will need to focus not just on their individual success, but the success of the entire ERG and especially their direct reports based on the ERG organization structure. And they will need to master budget allocation.

For these reasons, I have strong conviction that organizations owe an extra duty of care to help those individuals who step into the ERG leadership role without previous management or leadership experience. The new skills, time allocation, and work values that they need to master are significant. Without support from the organization, not only is it likely that the individual ERG leader will perform poorly, but so too will the entire employee resource group.

The three most effective ways to enhance the skills and capabilities of any ERG leader – and not just those who lack significant past leadership experience – is through coaching, ERG summits, and ERG leadership academies.

Individual ERG Coaching Sessions

Some organizations invest in specific coaching sessions with external ERG experts for the leaders of their employee resource groups. Ingredion Incorporated, an American multinational ingredient provider based in Illinois, invests in individual coaching sessions with the leadership teams of several of their business resource groups, which I provided. For example, coaching was provided to their disability ERG on establishing their core purpose and vision. Their Hispanic ERG leadership team was provided coaching on establishing their guiding principles and core pillars and defining their desired future state. Next, their multicultural ERG and I held several coaching sessions, mostly focused on how and when to effectively launch chapters globally. And finally, I coached their Women's ERG on the establishment of a measurement strategy to help them better define the impact they have on the organization. Each one of these coaching sessions was provided exclusively to the members of ERG leadership team to help in their professional growth and to help them enhance their governance of each group.

By investing in individual coaching for their business resource groups, Ingredion was enhancing the capability of their ERG leaders to establish and meet their goals. Their ERG leaders also were more engaged because they knew that the company was making an investment in them and helping them to be more effective. They realized that the coaching not only was helping them be better ERG leaders, but that the coaching was also benefiting their careers. The coaching allowed for a deeper level of learning as well, as the coaching was specific to a learning need related to serving on the ERG leadership team. By focusing on core ideology, key pillars, global expansion, and measurement strategy, Ingredion was better preparing their leaders to achieve ERG excellence. Other companies that invest in similar individual development coaching sessions for their employee resource groups include Liberty Mutual, Catalent Pharma, Uber, Abcam, and Facebook. For each of these companies, I have seen an improvement in the capabilities of their ERG leaders.

ERG Leadership Summits

Since about 2015, there has been a significant increase in the number of companies that now hold an annual leadership summit for their

ERG leaders. These summits run anywhere from four hours to four days. Some are huge events with hundreds of ERG participants from all over the world. This means ERG summits can rack up thousands of dollars in costs: airfare and accommodations for all the attendees, fees for outside speakers, production expenses, the many person-days that go into planning, and the enormous opportunity cost incurred by taking so many individuals away from their normal duties for a significant amount of time.

Yet, given all the cost and expenses incurred, companies still see the importance and value to having such ERG leadership summits. To convey just how prevalent ERG summits are, since 2015, I have helped design and have presented at ERG leadership summits for dozens of companies, ranging from Fortune 50 multinationals to small, nonprofit organizations. For example, I have been fortunate enough to participate as a keynote speaker at ERG leadership summits for such varied companies as MetLife, Under Armour, KPMG, Johnson Controls, VMware, Stanley Black & Decker, Port Authority of New York, SurveyMonkey, Micron Technology, National Credit Union Association, Fannie Mae, The Home Depot, Verizon, Raytheon Technologies, Zebra Technologies, MillerCoors, Northwestern Mutual, CBRE, Allstate, Federal Reserve Bank of San Francisco, Sanofi, Merck, Walgreens, and the National Basketball Association to name but a few.

If planned and executed properly, ERG leadership summits can serve as a powerful catalyst to align ERG leaders, develop solutions to problems, avoid derailers, introduce new strategies, and fuel collaboration across the employee resource groups. In my experience, the most impactful summits, and thus the most beneficial to the ERG leaders, are the ones that plan the event around the answers of two key questions: "What do we want the outcome of the summit to be from the perspective of the ERG leaders? and "What do you want ERG leaders to say when their ERG members ask, 'What happened at the summit?" Planning an ERG summit around gaining clarity on these two questions will lead to a more impactful leadership summit.

Additionally, ERG summits should not only allow for information to flow top down so that ERG leaders can capture the thinking of top executives, but they must also employ techniques and exercises that allow for upward communication from ERG leaders to senior management. At one ERG leadership summit, ERG leaders were able to convey to their executive sponsors and diversity leaders various thoughts, including: "We lack sufficient development," "Middle managers are not supporting us," "The budgeting process is not clear," and "Our ability to attract senior leaders as members is questionable." Allowing ERG leaders to share such sentiments and then developing strategies jointly to address them is a necessary component of an effective ERG leadership summit.

Finally, ERG summits should provide a chance for the ERG leaders to lay the groundwork for genuine collaboration after the summit. A summit may be the rare opportunity when all the ERG leaders get a chance to gather and get to know each other. Incorporate time on the summit agenda to not only provide updates on each ERGs' activities, but also allow them to share what each will be focusing on in the coming months to help create opportunities for collaboration. This further creates the conditions where ERG leaders have each other's back and helps to nurture a sense of camaraderie within this group of leaders.

Table 3.1 highlights the ERG Leadership Summit held in February 2021 by Catalent Pharma Solutions. I had the pleasure of presenting all three days of the virtual summit and was thoroughly impressed with the comprehensive and strategic approach taken for the ERG Leadership Summit. The summit includes:

- Active participation from the CEO
- Focus on the realities of Covid-19 impact on employee resource groups
- An external mental health expert speaking about the importance of expressing emotions in the workplace

Table 3.1 Catalent Pharma Solutions 2021 ERG Leadership Summit Agenda

Tuesday, February 9, 2021	Wednesday, February 10, 2021	Thursday, February 11, 2021
• CEO Welcome • 2020 ERG Year in Review • Mental Health Session – It's OK to Not be OK. (Sara Westbrook) **CULTURE** • Pandemic Impact on ERGs (Dr. Robert Rodriguez)	• Chief HR Officer Welcome • Intro to New DEI Global Director **CAREER** • Latino ERG Best Practice Sharing – ERGs and Talent Acquisition • Disability ERG Best Practice Sharing – Interviewing Candidates with a Disability **COMMUNITY** • LEARN-in-a-Box	**COMMERCE** • Diverse Supplier Global Program • Strategic Planning and 4C Assessment Results • Communications Best Practice – Sharing ERG Calendars **ERG RECOGNITION**

- A speaker from supplier diversity that further aligns ERG initiatives to business priorities, links ERG initiatives to the 4C Model, allows the ERGs to share best practices, and promotes collaboration by having employee resource groups share their calendar of upcoming initiatives, and even includes time to leader recognition

The summit proved to be immensely valuable to the ERG leaders and enhanced their ability to lead their ERGs more strategically.

ERG Leadership Academies

Can you afford the cost of poor ERG leadership? Unimpactful initiatives, disengaged members, leadership team turnover, bad decisions, unhappy executive sponsors, and no business impact? No, you can't. Thus, companies are realizing that it is more cost effective to invest in the development of their ERG leaders. ERG leaders have invested themselves by taking on the leadership role. By investing in leadership development, companies send a message to their ERG leaders that they care about them and want to help them succeed. Remember that ERG leaders can be nurtured and developed, but not wished into existence. It requires intentionality and purposeful professional growth.

A leadership academy establishes a formal program that aims to expand the capability for ERG leaders to perform and excel in their roles. The first step in establishing an ERG leadership academy is to define the ERG leadership needs. Think about any specific ERG leadership gaps that may exist. For example, if the employee resource groups are having difficulty establishing meaningful metrics to capture their impact, then a development session on effective measurement strategies would enhance their capability in this area. Think, too, about the ERGs short-term and long-term strategic goals. If, for example, several of your ERG leaders will be rotating out of their roles soon, a development success on leadership continuity and success planning would be justified.

Even the best leadership development academies and programs can't cultivate successful ERG leaders if you haven't clearly defined the ERG values and incorporated them into the leadership development program. For example, if you want your employee resource groups to think globally or to collaborate effectively, then include these topics into your ERG leadership academy. If you desire a high-performing ERG leadership team, then provide them development on how to become a high-performing team as opposed to hoping that it naturally happens.

At times, an organization can simply have their ERG leaders participate in development workshops that already exist within the company's learning and development function. Sure, ERG leaders can attend an existing workshop that discusses characteristics of a high-performing team that any employee can partake in. However, such general off-the-shelf training will likely miss some of the nuances specific to ERGs, such as including the fact that ERG leaders are volunteers, that ERG leaders have no formal authority over their teams, that their ERG responsibilities fall on top of their regular job responsibilities, and so on.

In my experience, an ERG leadership academy is much more effective because it provides professional and leadership development based specifically on their ERG leadership role. This means that the workshop topics, development scenarios, and session objectives are created with the ERG leader in mind.

It is also an excellent idea to have ERG leaders themselves articulate the desired topics for their developmental workshops. They are in the best position to indicate which areas would benefit them the most with regards to their development as an ERG leader. In spring of 2021, I worked with Uber Technologies Inc., the ride-hailing, food delivery, and freight transportation company based in Silicon Valley. Part of the engagement included the establishment of an ERG leadership academy for the leaders of their 11 global ERGs. Uber was emphatic that each potential workshop must be designed specifically for ERG leaders and take into consideration their important role within their ERGs.

When selecting the possible topics to address in each ERG workshop, with one workshop being delivered each quarter, the global diversity, inclusion, and equity team first reviewed the results of their recent 4C ERG Assessment. Some of the developmental workshops were selected based on the results of the assessment. Next, the ERG leaders were asked to identify the developmental workshops that most appealed to them or felt would be the most beneficial in helping them become even stronger ERG leaders. They were asked to identify their top choices for developmental workshops from a list of 12 possible topics (see Table 3.2). The result was the establishment of the Uber ERG Leadership Academy that began in the summer of 2021. The Uber Leadership Academy addressed the most pressing development needs of their ERG leaders. Equally important, the ERG Leadership Academy demonstrated a significant investment by Uber in helping to ensure success and effectiveness of their ERG leaders worldwide.

ERG Leader Competencies

What makes an effective ERG leader? I am often asked this question, along with what are the necessary capabilities and competencies that every ERG leadership should possess. This is difficult to answer succinctly because ERG leaders play such an important role. ERG leader competencies are the skills and behaviors that contribute to superior ERG performance and achieving ERG excellence. In my work with hundreds of corporations, having interacted with thousands of ERG leaders, and reviewing the results of my 4C ERG Assessment, I've now gained a comprehensive understanding of the competences that are present within the employee resource groups that demonstrate ERG excellence. But for now, I'm going to focus on two critically important capabilities – effective decision-making and the balancing of leadership priorities.

Effective Decision-Making

ERG leaders must be decisive and capable of applying different decision-making approaches based on a variety of scenarios. They must know when they alone should decide what to do based on their role as ERG leader and when it is best to allow others to make a decision

Table 3.2 UBER ERG Leadership Academy Development Workshop Topics

ERG Metrics-that-Matter Key aspects of an ERG measurement strategy, the establishment of scorecards, and review of the 50 most commonly used ERG metrics.	ERG Strategic Planning Insights on how to accurately assess ERG current state, develop a desired ERG future step, then effectively creating an ERG plan.	Strong ERG Leader Teams Key elements to establish highly effective ERG leadership teams. Inject healthy team dynamics in the DNA of an ERG.	Leaders Developing Leaders Enhance ERG succession planning and leadership continuity efforts. Grooming future ERG leaders.
Attracting ERG Allies Review how ERGs can create allies throughout the organization. Learn how to leverage allies as advocates and evangelists.	Key Executive Sponsor Roles Leverage your ERG executive sponsor via 6 key roles they can play. Strategies to strengthen your executive sponsor relationship.	Elevate ERG Business Impact Understand how your ERG can have greater alignment with company goals and business initiatives.	ERG Chapter Expansion Key considerations when establishing additional ERG chapters nationally or globally.
ERG Member Engagement 2.0 Increase member engagement via stronger ERG relevance. How to drive reciprocity within your ERG.	Avoiding ERG Derailers Most common ERG derailers and how to avoid them.	4C Model Best Practices External trends and best practices related to the use of the 4C ERG Model.	Professional Development Tips Key aspects of an ERG member professional development strategy.

that is in the best interest of the employee resource group. Some ERG leaders are effective at making decisions because they are methodical and use specific steps before making important decisions. Others just have an innate ability to understand the dynamics of buy-in and inclusiveness in determining how a decision should be made.

I'm not saying that effective ERG leaders always make the right decision; what I've seen is that effective ERG leaders demonstrate the willingness to be decisive. ERG leader decisiveness is key for effectively executing plans and achieving ERG goals. Decisiveness is one of those skills that ERGs don't often talk about, but it's extremely important to great ERG leadership. Just imagine an ERG leader who can't make up their mind and who is constantly asking others what they think, and even then is still never able to come to a conclusion.

I like decisive ERG leaders because they tend to do what they say they will do. This means they are responsible and accountable for their decisions. Decisive ERG leaders also convey confidence because they tend to couch every message with self-assurance. This self-assurance usually builds trust within the ERG and makes others want to follow. Decisiveness also means that an ERG leader will be quick to decide. They simply have the ability to decide with speed and clarity because they tend to trust their instincts.

Decisive ERG leaders tend to also be bold. Indecision itself is the root of much fear, stress, and worry. By being less fearful, decisive ERG leaders are more likely to take calculated risks. If an ERG leader does make a wrong decision, they treat it as a lesson – and they rarely repeat the same mistake. If I've noticed one thing within diversity and inclusion departments (who often have oversight over employee resource groups), it is that they dislike having indecisive ERG leaders who sit idly by and let things happen. So, if you want your employee resource groups to achieve excellence, develop effective decision-making skills and decisiveness in your ERG leaders.

Balancing Leadership Priorities

ERG leaders have many tasks to manage. They cannot afford to spend all of their time focusing on just one thing. So, the most effective ERG leaders must put their effort where it is most needed, whether that means getting their ERG leadership team on board with the ERG strategic plan or helping to groom his or her successor. While managing time and balancing priorities may sound simple in theory, it is infuriatingly difficult in practice because ERG leaders not only have to perform in their regular day job, but they are often bogged down in the day-to-day complexities of running the employee resource group. This creates a scenario where ERG leaders are "always-on" and have to perform and deliver results in a role that is often very visible to all ERG stakeholders. It is no wonder that many ERG leaders often have the feeling that there are simply not enough hours in a day to get everything done. At times I have recommended to ERG leaders who want to better manage their priorities to begin tracking and budgeting their time and attention as if it were money. An ERG leader's time is a limited resource and should be invested only in activities that enhance the achievement of ERG goals.

My good friend Angel Gomez, an executive coach and president of AG Consulting, always promotes the philosophy that the effectiveness of any ERG leader depends on their ability to align and balance three areas of focus; achieving objectives, controlling how the work gets done, and managing relationships among their fellow ERG colleagues. No longer is the achievement of ERG goals sufficient to be considered a good ERG leader. Successful ERG leaders balance the achievement of ERG goals with the necessity for efficient processes and the interpersonal relationships with their partners to accelerate overall collaboration and performance. Every leader must constantly find ways to shift and align priorities. As Angel Gomez says, "Good leaders get results for their employee resource group. But the best ERG leaders get things done well and efficiently, while maintaining healthy relationships with others."

Let's look at these three components separately. From a people perspective, ERG leaders must facilitate collaboration and effectively interact with others but also do so in a manner that fosters connection and builds trust. They must also complete their work in an environment where things are structured with clear and replicable processes in order to influence others to make things happen. Finally, they must strive to achieve ERG goals so that the ERG gains a sense of achievement. These three aspects (people, goals, procedures) must be managed with balance. Too much focus by an ERG leader on people and the goals of the employee resource group might not be met. An overreliance on procedures might make ERG members feel micromanaged. Or too great an emphasis on meeting ERG goals might cause the ERG not to follow necessary company procedures or protocols.

Balancing these three components requires discipline and development. That is why organizations must invest in development that will help their ERG leaders effectively balance their ERG leadership priorities. Otherwise, most ERG leaders will continue to find that there is a significant gap between their priorities for their employee resource group and the actual use of their time allocated to their ERG priorities.

Organizations should also recommend the following strategies to ERG leaders so they can better balance their priorities. First, ERG leaders should be reminded of the old adage, "It is better to underpromise and overdeliver." With this in mind, an ERG leader should identify no more than five strategic priorities for their employee resource group. They should connect with their leadership team to determine which ERG priorities are most important and which require the most time. Encourage ERG leaders to rank these key strategic drivers and then allocate parts of their schedule to each one based on importance. It's an age-old business maxim: the activities that get monitored and measured – and incentivized – get done. ERG leaders should be encouraged to set up a time-budgeting system that allows them to identify ERG priorities, define time goals for each, and then track how they are actually spending their time against the budget. With this system in place, ERG leadership can recalibrate and rebalance if priorities and time allocation corrections are misaligned.

Second, organizations should remind leaders of the importance of asking questions before dedicating time to one of their priorities. First, is the issue in question a key ERG strategic priority? If so, can the ERG leader's time positively impact the issue? Could someone else handle it just as well as, or better than, the ERG leader? If you answer yes to this last question, the ERG leader should delegate the task. Finally, does the leader need to act immediately? If more groundwork is needed, then the ERG leader should delegate it and invest their time only when the issue is ripe. Time management is a battle of determining when and when not to act. Successful ERG leaders don't step in unless they can make the biggest impact possible in the shortest amount of time.

Effectively balancing leadership priorities requires that ERG leaders *clearly define what is strategic and what isn't, with regards to what is best for the employee resource group*. Building relationships with the ERG executive sponsor is strategic. Creating a process to groom the next ERG leader is strategic. Visiting with business unit leaders and identifying ways the employee resource group can support the organization's goals is strategic. However, things like overseeing the ERG newsletter or helping to set up the next Zoom call are not priorities. Remind your ERG leaders to constantly keep in mind the things they deem strategic as well as those they don't. This reduces the risk of ERG leaders focusing on things that don't require the use of their intellectual capital.

ERG leaders should also be told that they shouldn't be afraid to say no. When an ERG leader has strategic priorities in place and has allocated energy to accomplish them, they should be ready to stick to it at all costs. This will often require them to turn down other things.

Turning down nonstrategic time and energy investments allows ERG leaders to focus on their most strategic activities.

The overall message of this chapter is not only to remind the reader of the importance of the ERG leader role but also to convey how challenging the role can be. Most ERG leaders inherently know the individual benefits they will receive, but it is a good idea to remind them to help keep them motivated. The hope is that by outlining these aspects, organizations will elevate the sense of urgency and priority in having a formalized strategy to meet the development needs of ERG leaders. Whether the development is delivered via coaching, a leadership summit, or through a formalized leadership academy, your ERGs are more likely to achieve excellence if you nurture your ERG leaders.

4 The 4C Model™

A Holistic Approach Toward ERG Excellence

The day is still fresh in my memory. It was summer of 2008 and my excitement level was high as I was launching one of my first consulting engagements. A Latina executive at Avon had invited me to one of company's office locations in downtown Manhattan to discuss how I might help the organization with their employee resource groups. My name had been given to her by Avon's chief diversity officer as someone who could help. She served as the executive sponsor for their Hispanic ERG, which was called AHORA.

During our initial discussion, she provided me with a historical perspective on AHORA and some of their past accomplishments. She felt that while the accomplishments were strong, there is still untapped potential within the group. From there, we began to explore various ways that AHORA could make an even greater impact on the organization. She described professional development workshops AHORA had sponsored in the past. Next, she shared how she was very proud of AHORA's community outreach and how they had supported several local nonprofits. She did feel that the employee resource group could do a better job of helping Avon sell more products within the Hispanic community. Avon had always wanted to gain a bigger piece of the Latina consumer market and she felt that AHORA could be well positioned to do so. Finally, we spoke about the upcoming Hispanic

Heritage Month and how AHORA usually held an event to highlight Hispanic culture.

We spoke of how AHORA was doing many great things. My recommendation at the time was that AHORA needed to identify some key pillars that would serve as the foundation of their work. In the past, they had used three pillars to anchor their ERG work – Workplace, Workforce, and Marketplace. The executive felt these pillars were fine but really didn't capture the broad scope of activities that AHORA focused on. Plus, she felt these three pillars were a bit confusing (and I agreed with her). So, we set upon identifying new pillars that would not only resonate with the Latino ERG but that would also better capture their universal approach. We landed on Career as a pillar to reference their professional development workshops, as AHORA wanted to accelerate the career advancement of their members. Community as a pillar made sense, as AHORA was involved in several community outreach efforts. Our meeting ended, and I promised the executive sponsor I'd help identify the remaining pillars so that AHORA could have a strategic framework to operate within.

On my flight back to Chicago that evening, I was brainstorming some ideas for names that would capture the other work of AHORA. In thinking about the upcoming Hispanic Heritage Month, my thought was that this effort was to help celebrate Latino culture. Culture resonated with me because it not only captured the focus on Hispanic culture, but AHORA was also trying to raise cultural awareness among non-Hispanic people. In thinking about other ERGs besides AHORA, they too were trying to elevate cultural awareness via their ERG initiatives. It was then that I decided that Culture would be the name of the third pillar I would recommend.

What was left were the ERG initiatives that currently fell under the Marketplace pillar. We could go with the four pillars of Culture, Community, Career, and Marketplace. But that seemed off. To me, it made sense to try to have each pillar begin with the same letter.

I thought to myself, if I could only land on a word that started with C to represent Marketplace, that would be terrific. Company came to mind, but it didn't necessary convey that AHORA wanted to help Avon sell more products to Latinas. Consumers might work, but this word only focused on the person buying the products, not necessarily on the process of trying to sell them the product. Then it occurred to me that my next business trip was to Lexington, Kentucky, where I was invited by the Hispanic Chamber of Commerce to give a keynote speech on the importance of the growing Hispanic purchasing power. And just like that, the magic word I was looking for emerged … Commerce. Commerce felt like just the right word for what AHORA was trying to do. AHORA was trying to increase the sale of more Avon products to Latinas. I now had the four pillars that would make a holistic value proposition for Avon – Career, Community, Culture, and Commerce.

During the follow-up call with the Latina executive at Avon, I shared with her the recommended framework for AHORA – the 4C Model, I called it. She loved it. It was catchy, easy to remember, and most importantly, captured the holistic value that AHORA provides to the Avon organization. And thus, the 4C Model was born (See Figure 4.1). Being the entrepreneur that I am, I quickly obtained the copyright to the 4C Model and got it trademarked because I thought it had great appeal and tremendous potential.

Since that humble beginning, the 4C Model™ has been embraced by over 300 companies as the strategic framework for their employee resource groups. And these are just the companies that have worked with me directly. Just about every month I learn of another company that uses the 4C Model, even though I have never worked with them directly. For example, in 2019 I attended an ERG Summit in Silicon Valley where I was a keynote speaker, and I addressed the topic of ERG metrics. Later that afternoon, the summit agenda indicated that someone from PayPal, the payment systems company based in

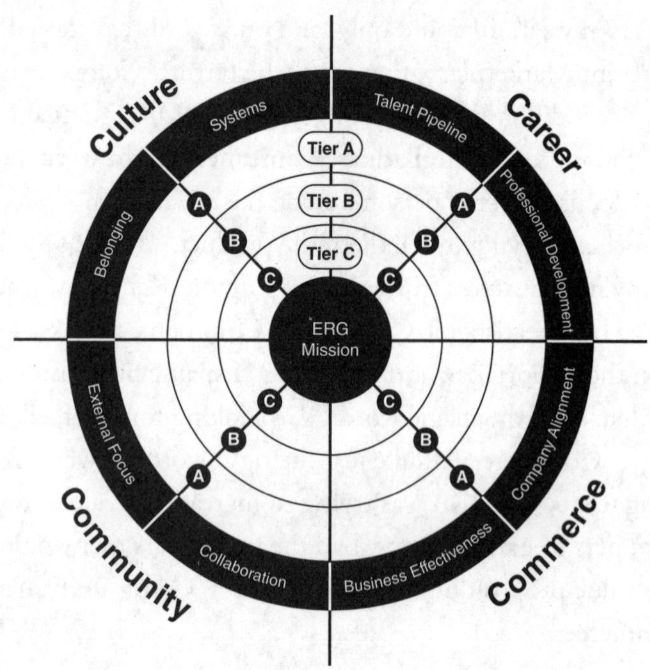

Figure 4.1 The 4C ERG MODEL™

San Jose, California, was going to speak about the company's employee resource groups. Having never worked with PayPal as a client before, I was curious about its ERGs. You can imagine my surprise when the PayPal speaker mentioned their use of the 4C Model as the strategic framework for all of their employee resource groups. Afterward, I introduced myself and shared that I was the creator of the 4C ERG Model. He shared that a PayPal employee had previously worked at a company that used the 4C Model. They liked the framework so much that they recommended to PayPal, who adopted it as their strategic framework.

To gain a sense of just how widespread the 4C Model is, consider this sample list of companies that use my 4C Model: Uber, Under Armour, Stanley Black & Decker, Ingredion, Liberty Mutual, LinkedIn, TJX Companies, Catalent Pharma, Verizon, Levi Strauss,

Astellas, Northwestern Mutual, Allstate, U.S. Cellular, SurveyMonkey, State Street, Biogen, Blue Cross Blue Shield, FiatChrysler, National Credit Union Administration, Herman Miller, ManpowerGroup, Tufts Health Plan, and Facebook, to name just a few corporations.

Because so many companies use the 4C Model, it would be fair to say that it is now the most widely used strategic framework for employee resource groups in corporate America. Personally, I am humbled by how well it has been received and am amazed that its popularity has grown since it was first applied by Avon over 10 years ago.

Over time, the 4C Model has evolved with minor tweaks being made as it relates to style, wording, and appearance. Figure 4.2 shows some of the past iterations of the 4C Model and includes its current form today on the far right.

Key Aspects of the 4C Model™

People often ask what has led to the huge acceptance of the 4C Model within organizations. One of the main reasons is because of the comprehensive nature it conveys related to employee resource groups. If an ERG is effectively able to make an impact in the areas of careers, community, culture, and commerce, that is a broad and wide-ranging value proposition.

Employee resource groups that embark on initiatives that address each of the 4C pillars are conveying to their organization that they see themselves as having the ability to support their company's diversity and inclusion efforts holistically. They are proclaiming that their ambitions are not narrow, nor are their aspirations meek. This is a bold declaration. It stirs the soul, and it inspires people to get involved. For ERGs that want to be perceived as brave, audacious, and gallant, what better way than to embrace the 4C Model.

Besides being comprehensive, the 4C Model is also balanced. The 4C Model is shaped like a circle to reflect this balance. The circular

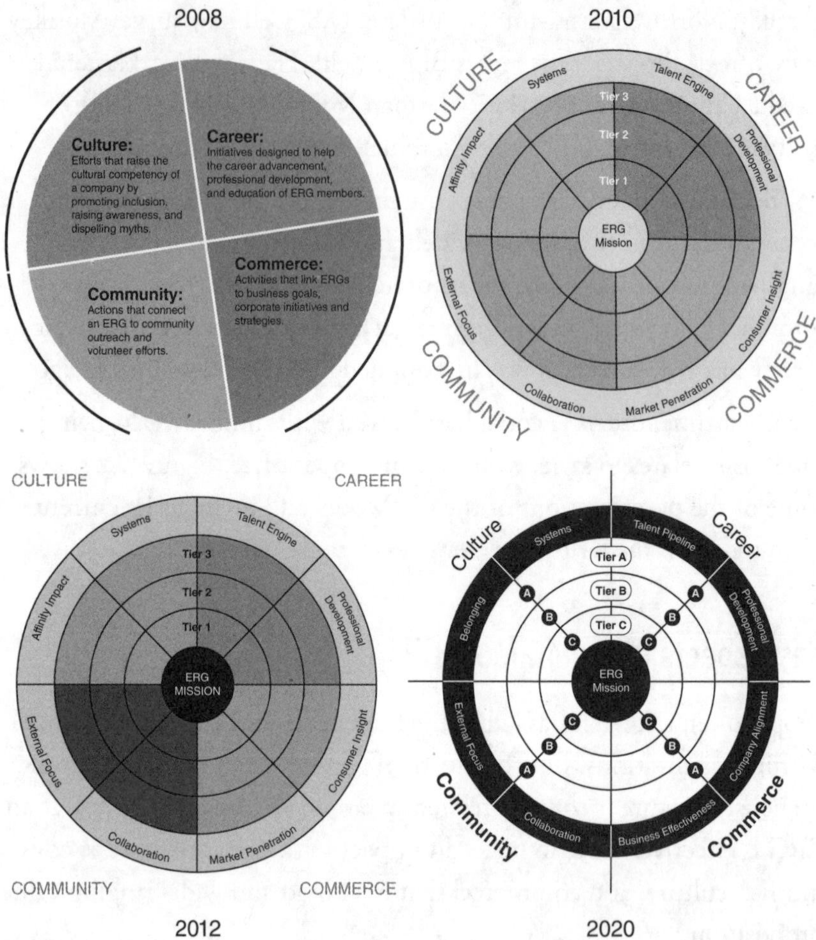

Figure 4.2 4C ERG Model™

nature of the model conveys that each of the 4C components is equally important. No one pillar is more important than another, and thus it communicates what an employee resource group is trying to accomplish. Similar to the balanced scorecard methodology related to measuring company performance, the 4C Model gives everyone a fast and comprehensive view of what ERGs are trying to accomplish.

While each of the 4C pillars can provide specific benefits individually, my experience has taught me that executives do not want to rely on just one of the 4C pillars at the exclusion of one of the other pillars. Diversity leaders and business executives want a balanced approach to be taken by their ERGs and the 4C Model conveys just that. Consider the balanced approach of the 4C Model like the indicators and gauges in an airplane instrument panel. To effectively fly and steer an airplane, pilots need to know about air speed, altitude, bearing, and destination. A pilot cannot rely on just one measure of performance. Similarly, those responsible for managing ERGs need to view the performance and effectiveness of their ERGs through several lenses simultaneously. Are the ERGs helping members with career advancement? Do they support community outreach efforts? Are ERGs elevating our cultural competency? Are they driving business results?

This imagery of a balanced approach to employee resource group value and impact is what the 4C Model provides.

Those companies that have embraced the 4C Model as the strategic framework for their employee resource groups have conveyed to me that this balanced approach meets several managerial needs. First, the 4C Model brings together, in a single framework, many of the organization's seemingly unrelated elements of their diversity strategy: accelerating career advancement for historically underrepresented minority groups, community outreach effectiveness, enhancing cultural competency, and linking diversity to business goals. The 4C Model conveys stability, security, equality, and forward movement to business leaders.

Second, the balanced 4C approach guards against suboptimization. By forcing stakeholders to consider all of the important ERG measures together, the 4C Model lets them see how everything is interconnected. The 4C approach aligns nicely with the balanced scorecard approached used by many organizations. This understanding can help transcend the traditional narrow perception of the past of what ERGs do and how they add value.

Oh, and let's not forget the name itself, the 4C Model™. It's short and easy to remember. As a way to convey Career, Community, Culture, and Commerce pillars, the 4C Model is an easygoing abbreviation used to convey the comprehensive aspirations for ERGs. By streamlining communications, the 4C Model makes it easy to define what ERGs are about. Plus, the 4C Model provides a strategic framework that organization leaders are accustomed to seeing and comprehending. Compared to the clumsy, hard-to-remember, difficult-to-define pillars of Workforce, Marketplace, and Workplace ERG model used by some companies, it is no wonder why the 4C Model has been embraced by so many organizations and in corporate America.

Using the 4C Model™

Besides serving as an effective strategic framework for ERGs, the 4C Model provides numerous benefits. First, it provides a wonderful basis for establishing the organizational structure of an ERG. Dozens of times I have seen an ERG have a committee for each of the 4C Pillars in their organizational structure. In such instances, they have a Career committee to oversee professional development initiatives and a Commerce committee to find ways to align ERG efforts with business goals. They then have a Community committee to guide the ERG's civic and local outreach plans. And as expected, they have a Culture committee to ensure some of their initiatives seek to raise cultural awareness within an organization.

Whether or not the ERGs use the framework as an outline for their organizational structure, the 4C Model makes it easy for ERGs to collaborate with each other. For example, I've seen many instances where those responsible for the culture initiatives within their ERG meet periodically with their counterparts within other ERGs who are also accountable for the culture related initiatives. By meeting and sharing updates on plans or upcoming projects with each other, ERGs are better able to partner and collaborate, thus reducing redundancies and avoiding a scenario where the ERGs operate in silos.

The rise in collaboration promoted by the 4C Model has led to an increase in ERG events that address the issue of intersectionality. Intersectionality looks at the interconnected nature of social categories such as race, gender, and ethnicity as they apply to individual ERGs. One such example of an intersectionality event I participated in occurred during Hispanic Heritage Month in 2020. Here, the Hispanic ERG at Facebook, called Latin@, reached out to me to facilitate a panel. Latin@ was partnering with Facebook's Black ERG, called Black@, on an intersectionality event that focused on the experiences of Afro-Latinos in the workplace. The panel session was a tremendous success for both employee resource groups, as it not only raised awareness about issues affecting Afro-Latinos, it showed how the Latin@ and Black@ ERGs were able to leverage the 4C Model to facilitate such a collaboration that focused on the intersectionality of the two groups.

Besides serving as a guide for organizational structural purposes and helping to promote increased collaboration, the most widely used application of the 4C Model is that it helps an ERG with prioritization. I will be the first to admit that while the 4C Model advocates that ERGs address each of the 4C pillars equally, it is not easy to accomplish within a typical one-year cycle. So, while an ERG may strive to address all 4Cs, they often need to prioritize. The 4C Model thus provides ERGs a mechanism to help with this prioritization. This is important because it allows ERGs to give attention to tasks that are urgently needed at the moment while acknowledging that they will focus on other areas at a later time. Sometime a change in ERG leadership pushes for a change in priorities for a group. Other times external factors create a shift in priorities such as reduced ERG budgets or requests that ERGs support special, time-critical initiatives.

The 4C Model thus helps ERGs prioritize their efforts by allowing them to weigh urgency versus importance. Approaching deadlines may require an ERG to put off other things in order to get something done before it is too late. However, if something critically important arises suddenly, it is prudent for ERGs to focus on something vital even if it wasn't planned for ahead of time. The 4C Model thus helps an ERG with evaluating the urgency and importance of something that requires priority.

The best example of this was what occurred with many of the ERGs when the Covid-19 pandemic hit in spring of 2020. Suddenly, ERGs had members who began working from home. ERG members who were parents now had to work from home while also watching their children, whose classes had all been moved online. Take all the stress from the pandemic, add to it the strain of economic uncertainty, plus the tension of a polarized election cycle, the isolation of possibly living alone, and on top of that the racial protests that were happening due to the George Floyd incident, and ERGs abruptly had to change their plans and adjust their priorities.

Career-related initiatives and Commerce-linked initiatives were seen as less important to many ERG leadership teams for the time being. Of increased importance became maintaining a sense of Community with ERG members who were now dispersed and not all in the same office location. Employee resource groups elevated the importance of initiatives aimed at helping their members dealing with anxiety, depression, wellness, and mental health issues. Within the 4C Model construct, Career and Commerce initiatives took a back seat to Culture and Community initiatives for ERGs across the country. Again, the 4C Model helped ERGs adjust their priorities and convey those priorities to others using the familiarity of a common framework and language.

Application of the 4C Model provides another way for companies to utilize the model to help drive certain approaches to be used by their ERGs. For example, a national retail organization based in the suburbs of Boston, Massachusetts, was adamant that each of their six employee resource groups should have at least one key initiative in each of the 4C pillars each year. The company thus has each ERG focus on a different 4C pillar each quarter. Each ERG can determine which pillar they will focus on each of the four quarters, but they must assign a different 4C pillar every quarter. By taking this approach, the company is driving each of its ERGs to have a well-rounded set of initiatives each year. Table 4.1 shows how their Veterans ERG assigned their initiatives quarterly. After one year, the Veterans ERG was proud of their ability to address each of the 4C pillars, thus solidifying their reputation as a well-rounded ERG that applies a balanced approach to adding value to the organization and its membership.

Another organization, a financial services company based in Illinois, takes a divide-and-conquer approach with applying the 4C ERG Model. The company has each ERG select one 4C pillar that they will focus on over the course of the year. Each ERG will place most of their emphasis on their selected 4C pillar for the entire year. The diversity and inclusion department then makes sure that each of the 4C pillars is represented by at least one of their employee resource groups. Each ERG can have initiatives in one of the other 4C pillars, but they are encouraged to mostly focus on the one assigned pillar for the year. The ERGs are assigned each of the 4C pillars over a four-year period so that an ERG can have a deep insight into a specific pillar on a four-year cycle. The ERGs are then instructed to share their initiatives in their main pillar with the other ERGs to identify ways to partner

Table 4.1 Veterans ERG Yearly Initiatives
Different 4C Pillar Focus Each Quarter

Q1 Jan.–March	Q2 April–June	Q3 July–Sept.	Q4 Oct.–Dec.
Career Pillar	**Community Pillar**	**Commerce Pillar**	**Culture Pillar**
• Launch mentoring circles	• Partner with HR organization to select key veteran nonprofit partner organization.	• Drive support of active military personal to buy back-to-school products for their children from company with discount code.	• Support talent acquisition efforts to hire more veterans.
• Professional development workshop on conveying executive presence.	• Organize event to place American flags at grave sites of military veterans on Memorial Day.	• Work with supplier diversity to identify more veteran-owned businesses as vendors.	• Intersectionality event with LGBTQ ERG on being gay in the military.

and collaborate. For example, the Women's ERG was assigned to focus mostly on the Career pillar. But all their Career pillar initiatives were then open to members of all the other ERGs. Similarly, Disability ERG focused on the Community pillar, but members from every ERG were invited to support and participant in their community initiatives.

Table 4.2 shows how the 4C pillars were assigned to their eight employee resource groups. By utilizing the 4C Model in this manner,

Table 4.2 Assigned 4C Pillars by Employee Resource Group

Career Pillar	Culture Pillar	Commerce Pillar	Community Pillar
• Women's ERG • Young Professionals ERG	• Veterans ERG • Black ERG	• Hispanic ERG • LGTBQ ERG	• Disability ERG • Asian-American ERG

the company is promoting an ERG strategy focused more so on depth than breadth. This approach allows ERGs to gain a deep level of understanding about a specific pillar and how it benefits their membership. Plus, the ERG can allocate their resources and energy on the one pillar, thus investing more in that specific pillar as opposed to having to spread that energy and budget over 4 pillars each and every year. By having an ERG focus mainly on one 4C pillar, the ERGs can develop initiatives that have a significant impact on each of the pillars.

As the creator of the 4C ERG Model™, I don't really advocate for any one approach over another on how an organization should apply the model. I understand the benefits of an approach that assigns a different 4C pillar per quarter as much as I do in assigning one pillar per ERG per year. To me, I can also see why having a more hands-off approach and allowing the ERGs to decide how to leverage the 4C model on their own makes sense. That's part of the beauty of the 4C Model: organizations can apply the model in the manner that suits them best. To be clear, however, I do believe that ERG excellence requires that an ERG address each of the 4C pillars over time. The length of that time duration is up to an organization and to the ERG. By doing so, ERGs can establish the holistic value proposition that ERG excellence calls for.

If you take a close look at the 4C Model, you will notice that at the very center is ERG Mission. That is because ERG excellence requires that initiatives undertaken by ERGs should be aligned with the mission of the ERG. The mission of any ERG defines its fundamental reason for existing. The mission conveys why the ERG exists and reflects the ERGs idealistic motivation for the work that it does. And while the 4C Model has evolved and changed slightly over time, ERG Mission has already remained at the center, serving as the anchor that brings the 4C pillars together. What this means is that the mission of an ERG should have timeless character. The strategies and practices of the ERG may change, but the ERG mission should not. The 4C Model reflects this.

Placing ERG Mission at the center of the 4C Model also conveys a sense of authenticity that should exist within the ERG. An ERG does not invent or create their core mission; they discover it by looking inward. Ultimately, the primary role of the ERG mission is to guide and inspire the ERG stakeholders. By placing ERG mission at the center of the 4C Model, ERG members are inspired to accomplish their 4C initiatives with distinction so that the mission of the ERG is achieved.

All this is not to say that the 4C Model does not have its critics. Some say that the model is confusing and that it intuitively does not always allow for easy categorization of their initiatives. For example, should ERG efforts that support diversity recruiting be placed in the Culture pillar, the Community pillar, or the Commerce pillar? Some believe it is impossible to categorize every ERG initiative into only four pillars. Others believe the 4C Model is too gimmicky. By this they mean that the 4C Model is designed primarily to attract attention, but that the model itself has little intrinsic value. Some people simply don't like the color or the shape of the 4C Model. I guess you can't please everyone. There is also a diagnostic and ERG assessment component associated with the 4C Model, but we will cover that in detail in Chapter 9.

So, there it is, the 4C Model. I consider it my gift to employee resource groups around the world. The 4C Model also allows me to give back to ERGs for all that they did for me when I was early in my career. Besides taking great pride in seeing my 4C Model be utilized globally, it was especially rewarding to see the 4C Model highlighted as part of a Harvard Business School case study in *Harvard Business Review* in August 2020, written by my friend Amy Hernandez Turcios and the esteemed Harvard professor Rosabeth Moss Kanter. Now the 4C Model is utilized in one of the top business schools in the world to teach students about the power of ERGs.

To me, the 4C Model™ will be part of my legacy. I hope that even when I'm gone, the 4C Model will continue to exist. If so, it will show that it can stand the test of time and that the 4C Model is not restricted to a particular period of time. While the 4C Model definitely has a beginning, there is optimism that it will never have an end. I designed the 4C Model to be eternal – or if not eternal, to at least be ageless and relevant for a very long time. The next four chapters will each do a deep dive into each of the 4C pillars so that readers gain a greater understanding of what each pillar represents and how ERGs can leverage each pillar in their pursuit of excellence.

5 Career Pillar

Turning ERGs into a Talent Engine

The competition had been fierce, and the top five finalists felt honored to be in such an elite group of companies. It was September 2010, and the United States Hispanic Chamber of Commerce (USHCC) had just launched the Latino ERG Corporate Challenge in an effort to identify the best Latino ERG in the country. A stellar group of judges had reviewed dozens of submissions from leading Latino ERGs across the country. The finalists had been invited to the USHCC convention in Dallas to present their case for why they should receive the trophy.

Two hundred Latino ERG representatives witnessed HACEMOS, the Latino employee group from AT&T, take the top prize. The winning quality? AT&T had turned HACEMOS into a talent engine with both current and future organizational leaders actively engaged in running the ERG.

A year later, at the USHCC conference in Miami, there was a new Latino ERG Corporate Challenge winner: General Electric's Hispanic Forum. But the winning quality was the same: GE's Hispanic Forum had been able to attract top corporate executives into the ERG. Both the 2010 and 2011 winners proved that ERG leadership roles can be the key to not only achieving tremendous success for individuals and the ERG itself, but to also sustaining, replicating, and scaling ERG success across the enterprise.

The key message that was sent by GE and AT&T, almost like a shot fired across the bow of other ERGs, was the realization that ERGs need to make themselves a destination for current corporate leaders and a talent incubator of future ones.

Unfortunately, what AT&T and GE have been able to achieve was, at the time, still the exception when it comes to ERGs. Today, the demand for leaders greatly exceeds the supply. Look at the membership roster of most ERGs, and you'll find job titles of employees who are mostly individual contributors and specialists. Occasionally, you'll see a member who is a manager, and even more rare, a member who has achieved the level of director. For employees at the director level and above, ERGs simply are not seen as relevant.

ERGs have grown in sophistication and become more global, and most are now tasked with having a stronger alignment with business and marketplace goals. These are just some of the indicators that show that ERGs need an influx of top talent. The challenge for an organization is to create employee resource groups that will attract senior-level members who have stronger leadership capabilities and possess the ability to build teams and implement a strategy.

What's needed, therefore, is an approach that will allow organizations to turn their ERGs into a destination for seasoned leaders looking for growth experiences in diversity. There is a growing realization that to be an effective contemporary leader in an increasingly multicultural and global world, one needs to have firsthand experience with managing diversity in a savvy and effective way. That is where the Career pillar comes in (See Figure 5.1).

In my experience, the Career pillar is the one that tends to attract most ERG members. Employees often join an ERG because they want increased visibility, capability, and ultimately, increased promotability. While the other three pillars of the 4C Model are focused on work

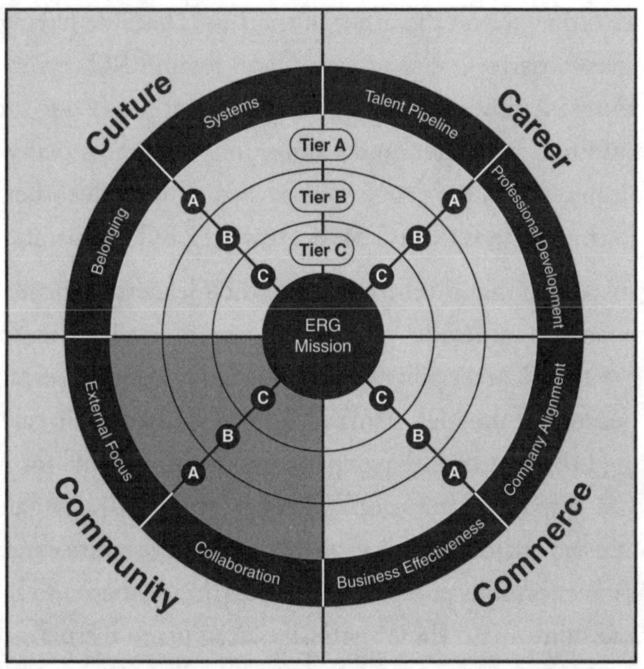

Figure 5.1 The Career 4C pillar.

environment, business goals, and the communal aspects of work life, the Career pillar is most associated with individual professional development.

Largely because the Career pillar is the main reason many join an employee resource group, our research shows that ERGs allocate most of their budget resources and initiatives on career-related efforts. In fact, an analysis of results from the 4C Assessment show that those ERGs that tend to have sustainable long-term success allocate about 40 percent of their budget and initiatives on the Career pillar and the remaining 60 percent allocated to the Culture, Community, and Commerce pillars almost equally. ERGs that want to remain relevant to their members are well served by ensuring they provide initiatives within the Career pillar. This is not to say that the Career pillar is more important than the other pillars but rather that this pillar has the greatest influence on the other three. This is because having strong Career pillar initiatives helps to attract and retain ERG members. With a strong membership base, ERGs are better situated to create and launch Culture, Commerce, and Community programs that will be impactful. In essence, the Career pillar helps to drive the other three pillars and thus propels the 4C Model toward ERG excellence.

Organizations that want to diversify their leadership teams with more women and minorities also tend to be strong advocates for ERGs investing in their Career pillars. I've seen many executive search firms flourish because of the high demand for diverse leadership talent. Consulting firms like mine have spent a great deal of time formulating a strategy to help companies cope with the "war for diverse talent." Just about every major organization is attempting to hire external stars offering enormous compensation to entice the best and brightest women and minorities. These aggressive attempts to recruit outsiders suggest that their internal leadership pipeline initiatives for diverse talent is inadequate. Their internal mentoring, training, and other developmental programs aren't keeping the pipeline full, making it necessary to look outside. What's needed, therefore, is an approach that will allow organizations to keep their own leadership pipelines full and flowing. By enhancing the leadership capabilities and promotional velocity of their membership, ERGs help to fill the talent pipeline with diverse talent that is upwardly mobile. And this is done mostly through the Career pillar initiatives.

The population in the United States is going to have an increasingly diverse identity in the immediate future. This means that organizations are going to have to meet the needs and demands of a society that is going to be more diverse tomorrow than it is today. To effectively connect with these diverse consumers, organizations must have a leadership profile that mirrors the communities that they are trying to serve. This means more women and historically underrepresented minorities in leadership positions. If executed well, the Career pillar helps to develop this next generation of diverse talent for an organization. Globally, organizations have become aware of the need for local leadership because of increasing globalization. Strategies coming from a US-based home office require local interpretation and application. Therefore, companies need leaders rooted in their local countries because they understand local issues and differences in culture, customer demands, and work environments. Because ERGs are now expanding globally, they are helping to fill the pipeline with bicultural talent that has a global mindset.

The problem is that many organizations do not look at their ERGs as part of their talent pipeline development initiatives, particularly those that still view ERGs as the "food, flag, and fun folks." Because of this lack of acknowledgment of the role of ERGs in diverse talent development, diversity departments, the HR function, and business leaders don't invest their time in providing oversight to the Career related initiatives of their ERGs. The results are often professional development initiatives within ERGs that are not strategic or organized with a specific purpose in mind.

Another benefit that ERGs provide that organizations fail to recognize is an ERG's ability to create more inclusive leaders. If our organizations are indeed becoming more diverse and more global, we must have leaders who can effectively guide and manage this workforce. When employees join an employee resource group as an ally, they are immediately enhancing their professional capabilities as an inclusive leader. Consider the inclusive insights gained by men who are active participants in a Women's ERG. Similarly, when an able-bodied person joins an ERG focused on disabilities they gain a new appreciation and broader perspective of the workplace experience for employees with a visual or hidden disability. The inclusive nature of ERGs is calling for more allies to join. As ally membership in ERGs grows, the organization benefits via the development of a pipeline with more inclusive leaders. Yet, a full-throttle endorsement by top corporate executives to rally more allies to join ERGs is unfortunately still the exception, not the norm. The time has come for organizations to recognize the untapped leadership development potential that exists within ERGs. This potential can be leveraged most directly through the Career pillar within the 4C Model.

We divide initiatives within the Career pillar into two segments, professional development and talent pipeline. While similar, these two segments are quite distinct. The professional development segment includes efforts designed to improve individual member capability. This tends to focus mostly on providing various professional development workshops. In contrast, talent pipeline efforts are more focused on accelerating the upward mobility of ERG membership. A slight distinction, perhaps, but further exploration of each will help to differentiate the two.

Professional Development

The most direct way that ERGs can meet the Career pillar expectations of their membership is to offer professional and leadership development workshops. Some of the most common workshops ERGs tend to offer to their members include sessions on a variety of topics such as communication skills, problem solving, conflict management, resume writing, personal branding, decision-making, effective teams, public speaking, project management, executive presence, and business writing. Often, an ERG can leverage existing professional development workshops that are already offered by their organization. In doing so, the ERGs are simply encouraging their membership to take advantage of existing professional workshops and resources that the ERG members may not have known existed or that they could participate.

It is not uncommon for ERGs to bring in external speakers to deliver professional development workshops for their membership.

I've personally delivered hundreds of such workshops to ERGs at companies in various industries. Some of the most common workshops I've delivered for ERGs include creating high-performance teams, authentic leadership, inclusive decision-making, balancing leadership priorities, coaching others, effective networking, conveying executive presence, and many, many more.

As ERGs look to provide solid professional development programming for their members, there are a few very important considerations to keep in mind. First is to put some thought into what types of professional development is most in need or desired by ERG membership. Some proactive ERGs will often survey or ask their membership what professional development topics they desire. Because the membership provides input into the topics, they tend to have greater buy-in and, thus, tend to participate in greater numbers when these workshops are provided. One caveat to this approach, however, is that ERG members must often identify potential leadership development workshops from a broad list of suggested topics. Employees are notorious for recommending development topics that they think they will like as opposed to advocating for development topics that they need. The result is often an ad hoc approach to professional development and hence a hodgepodge of offerings that are not aligned, thus limiting their impact on enhanced leadership growth.

A smarter move, in my opinion, is to have the ERG partner with the learning and development function at their organization in helping to identify professional development gaps and solutions. This tends to provide several benefits. First, learning and development can share existing professional development content and workshops that the ERG membership can simply participate in. This tends to minimize ERGs having to pay external speakers for professional development workshops that already exist. The second benefit is that the learning and development function can also conduct a more thorough needs analysis of ERG development requirements and deficiencies. Through a variety of methods, the learning and development function can gain insights into skills gaps that ERG members may have and recommend professional development workshops that close those gaps. Learning and development professionals can also help an ERG prioritize their professional development offerings with emphasis being placed on those topics that are most in need among the membership. Another benefit is that learning and development professionals are skilled at evaluating workshops after they have been delivered. This capability can help an ERG determine which workshops are really resonating with the membership and which are not. Finally, ERGs can learn how to capture the return on investment and maximize their professional development budgets if they partner with the learning and development function.

Being more intentional and strategic in meeting professional development expectations is a key capability for ERGs. Without a well-thought-out approach, ERGs run the risk of providing workshops in a manner where the topics selected may sound good, but do not follow any clear rationale or purpose. When this happens, ERGs run the risk of low member participation, poorly delivered or conceived workshops, or workshops that simply do not really help members gain new skills and capabilities. This further tends to erode the potential of ERGs being seen as a valuable resource in a company's leadership pipeline efforts.

In my experience, ERGs demonstrate excellence in the area of professional development when they realize that they need to provide workshops and content that appeals to members at various stages of their career. This is important because a workshop that might appeal to an ERG member who is an individual contributor will likely not appeal to an ERG member who is already a manager or director. Achieving ERG excellence thus requires ERGs to offer professional development content to members across the career continuum.

Career Pillar Case Study Side Bar

Several years ago, I worked with a pharmaceutical company whose ERGs were struggling to offer compelling professional development workshops for their membership. They asked for my help in working with their ERGs to take a more strategic approach to their professional development offerings. In meeting with the ERGs and probing into their membership profiles, a clear gap was discovered. The ERGs had done an effective job of attracting members from various job levels – or career stages, as they called them. They not only had a large number of members who were individual contributors (Stage 1), but many were also supervisors or managers (Stage 2). They also had several members who were directors (Stage 3), and some were even at vice president and executive levels (Stage 4) – see Figure 5.2.

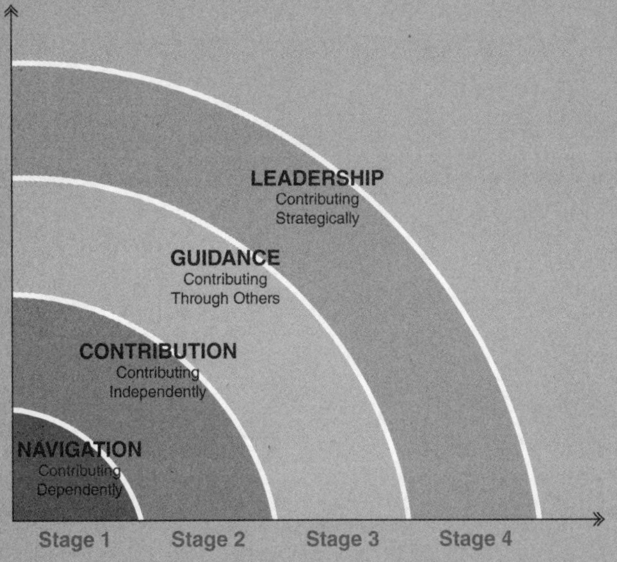

Figure 5.2 Professional development offerings per career stage.

(continued)

In analyzing their past professional development offerings, it quickly became apparent that almost all their workshops were most applicable to their members who were individual contributors or considered at Stage 1 of their careers. While this was great for their individual contributors, these workshops provided very little value, and were not appealing, to those members who were managers, directors, and vice presidents. With my guidance, the ERGs adopted a more sophisticated approach to their professional development planning by ensuring that their offerings appealed to members at a variety of job levels. They reduced the number of workshops delivered mostly for individual contributors such as resume writing and effective communication skills. In their place, they added more offerings on coaching others and giving feedback. These professional development workshops were more attractive to their members who were supervisors and managers or those considered to be at Stage 2 of their careers.

The ERGs also added workshops on leading high-performing teams and conveying executive presence. These workshops were well attended by the ERG members who were at Stage 3 and mostly held roles with the title of the director. And finally, we partnered with the learning and development department to recommend workshops that the ERGs could provide that would target vice presidents and executives, or those deemed to be at Stage 4. Our solution was to select an external speaker whose expertise was on helping individuals get selected onto highly visible nonprofit boards such as the local boards of the ballet, opera, art institute, and symphony. Such nonprofit boards are highly desired and coveted by corporate executives. The ERGs collaborated and pooled their funds so that they could jointly be responsible for delivering this particular workshop. During the actual workshop, ERG members were amazed at how many senior leaders and executives attended. These leaders not only attended, but several also became members of the ERG or became more active members.

This conveys ERG excellence because the ERGs at this company now had a more strategic approach that focused on providing professional development content to employees and members across the career continuum. This approach bolsters an ERG's ability to meet leadership pipeline needs and positions an ERG as a talent engine for the organization. A sign of ERG excellence indeed.

Other common initiatives that fall under the professional development segment include things such as leadership book series. This is when an ERG will select a leadership book and provide hard or electronic copies of the book to their membership who are encouraged to read the book. ERG members are then usually invited to a facilitated session where the participants are asked to share their thoughts and reflections on the book. ERG-facilitated book clubs help members gain new perspectives on the key themes of the book, improve communication skills, push members to read a book they might not otherwise read, and promote learning in an informal environment. Such efforts usually support professional development.

At times, ERGs will help fund participation of a few of their members to participate in external conferences or leadership development workshops. Afterward, the participating ERG members are asked to share with the rest of their ERGs their key insights, lessons learned, and new capabilities in an effort to extend the benefits of the external conference or workshop with a broader group of members. The premier US ERG conference is called EmERGe, which is organized by the organization Diversity Best Practices. This conference brings ERG and employee network groups from all industry sectors together to share effective practices to participate in professional development. Several hundred people attend each time the conference is offered. I have had the distinct privilege and honor to have attended, spoken at, or participated as a panelist at over a dozen of these ERG conferences and highly recommend that organizations send their ERG leaders and stakeholders.

In an effort to promote ERG professional development, some ERGs will arrange for their members to be given access to various personality or behavioral assessments supported by their organization such as the Myers-Briggs Type Indicator, Clifton StrengthsFinder, or DiSC Profile. Once taken, ERG members can gain insights into their strengths, potential weaknesses, preferred communication approach, and leadership tendencies. Once ERG members have taken their individual assessment, they usually attend professional development workshops sponsored by the ERG to help them interpret the results and identify strategies to act based on their assessment findings.

Talent Pipeline

The ERG initiatives that fall under talent pipeline usually are provided to members via a broader set of mechanisms. Unlike professional development offerings that tend to focus on workshops that are delivered in-person or virtually, talent pipeline efforts are more subtle but equally impactful. Also, professional development workshops tend to focus on new skill acquisition. Talent pipeline efforts are more focused on a member's upward career mobility.

For example, ERG efforts that result in increased visibility and exposure to executives are considered talent pipeline initiatives. Raising ERG members' visibility with executives provides an opportunity for them to appear on the radar of senior leaders. This exposure and visibility might not happen were it not for the members involvement in an ERG. The leaders of the ERGs tend to gain the most visibility and exposure to executives. This is because they are often the main contact for the executive sponsor of the ERG. This usually involves meeting periodically with a senior executive to provide updates on the status of the ERG or to share the strategic plans for the ERG.

What many ERG leaders have come to realize is that being good at your job is not the only requisite for getting ahead in one's career. If key executives and leaders are not aware of who you are, you are less likely to be considered for key assignments or promotional opportunities. Most ERG leaders have figured out that increased visibility with senior leaders maximizes their exposure, which could lead to higher consideration when opportunities arise. Due to Covid-19 and the fact that more employees now work from home, this increased visibility is invaluable. For those ERG leaders who feel uncomfortable with promoting themselves or are not naturally outgoing, the leadership role allows them to take a more active role in increasing their visibility.

What increased visibility provides to ERG leaders and members is a greater opportunity to demonstrate one's knowledge and expertise. ERG leaders often comment on how this role increased their self-confidence and helped them gain a level of comfort in interacting with top executives. ERGs thus provide a mechanism to help raise their awareness, enhance their reputation, and demonstrate their talents. These benefits often prove critical when key appointments and promotions are being determined and, thus, highlight how an ERG can help with upward career mobility and promotional velocity.

Along with increased exposure, ERGs also support talent pipeline efforts when they offer mentoring initiatives. Whether it's getting their members to participate in a company's existing mentoring program or it involves creating a separate mentoring program for their members, ERGs further help to build the talent pipeline. The benefits that mentors provide are well documented. Mentors usually offer career advice, serve as role models, provide emotional support, share feedback, help a mentee navigate corporate culture, and tend to focus on the mentees' personal and professional growth. When ERGs offer mentorship opportunities, they are helping their members with their career advancement.

At times, mentoring initiatives take on a unique twist. Several years ago, I was involved in a two-year engagement with Northwestern Mutual, the financial services and insurance company based on Milwaukee, Wisconsin. The engagement involved supporting their ERGs and contained several components. One particular component involved their Black/African American ERG launching of a reverse mentoring program. This program involved matching specific members of the Black ERG with top leaders at the company. Most mentoring programs are designed to have the senior leader provide guidance and mentoring to a more junior-level employee. In this reverse mentoring program, the main goal was for the member of the Black ERG to help the senior leader gain a better understanding of what it was like to work at the company as a Black employee. This proved to be a win–win initiative. The company executive gained unique insights that helped them be an even more inclusive leader and the Black ERG member gained valuable executive exposure.

Another talent pipeline initiative involves having ERGs provide greater insights into a company's leadership pipeline and talent management processes. For example, in 2021, I worked with one of the ERGs for a North American automotive company with headquarters in Texas. The engagement was aimed at helping to accelerate career advancement for ERG members. The result of the engagement was a three-part series for their ERG members. The first part focused on understanding the leadership pipeline process and how to effectively handle career pivot points. This first part of the engagement focused on providing ERG members greater clarity on how to prepare for continued upward career mobility. For example, ERG members were informed about how to move up in the leadership pipeline by going from being an individual contributor to being promoted to a manager role. Outlined were the key differences between individual contributor roles and manager roles, including how ERG members needed to leverage different skills, how their time needed to be allocated differently, and how their work values needed to shift – see Table 5.1. Similar content was shared on how to move from being a manager to being a director and moving from being a director to becoming a vice president.

The second part of the engagement focused on helping ERG members understand how talent management programs typically work. For example, they studied a common practice used by many organizations regarding how an employee is managed based on where an employee falls on the commonly used performance versus potential grid (see Figure 5.3). For example, employees learned that someone who is deemed a high performer but with low potential for upward mobility is managed differently from a talent perspective than someone who is considered to have high potential but is only a moderate performer.

The third part of the engagement looked at the phenomenon within companies in that many members of historically underrepresented groups are overmentored and undersponsored. While mentorship provides an employee with many benefits, what employees really need is an executive to advocate on their behalf by serving as a sponsor. This led to a session that focused on the differences between a

Table 5.1 North American Automotive Company Talent Pipeline Sessions for ERG Members Leadership Pipeline Career Pivots

Individual Contributor	First-Time Manager
Skills	Skills
• Technical proficiency • Team play • Relationship building • Following rules, processes, and procedures	• Planning work of others • Coaching • Assessing performance • Defining expectations • Communication • People selection
Time Application	Time Application
• Daily discipline • Meet personal due dates	• Annual planning • Time available for subordinates • Set priorities for unit and team • Communication time with other business units, customers, and suppliers
Work Values	Work Values
• Getting results through personal proficiency • High-quality technical work • Punctuality, content, quality, and reliability	• Getting results through others • Success of direct reports • Managerial work • Success of work unit • Visible integrity

mentor and a sponsor on how to leverage each to help accelerate career advancement (see Table 5.2).

The overall evaluations given by the ERG members of this three-part engagement were extremely high. Furthermore, many ERG members indicated that not only did they learn a lot about career

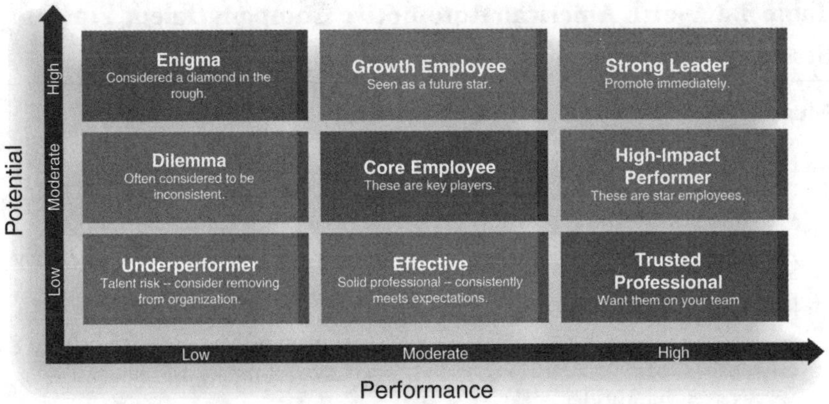

Figure 5.3 North American automotive company talent pipeline session for ERG leaders performance vs. potential.

advancement, but they also planned to apply the concepts they learned immediately to help improve their chances of promotion. All were grateful to the ERG for providing content focused on their upward mobility. The approach taken by the ERG at this organization is a clear example of how an emphasis on the Career pillar can support talent pipeline initiatives.

Career planning initiatives also promote talent pipeline efforts within the Career pillar. These efforts often include senior-level executives sharing their career path trajectory with members of an ERG. For example, an executive might discuss how having an international assignment accelerated their career advancement. Such insight might encourage an ERG member to pursue an international assignment. Others might describe how working with an external executive coach helped them develop the skills they needed to land a coveted promotion. Again, hearing an executive talk about the benefits of having an executive coach might encourage an ERG member to obtain a coach to help with their career advancement. Or a more senior leader might describe how their past experience as an ERG leader increased their visibility and exposure, and might influence a hesitant ERG member

Table 5.2 North American Automotive Company Talent Pipeline Session for ERG Members Mentors vs. Sponsors

Mentor	Sponsor
• Can sit at any job level • Provides emotional support • Gives feedback on how to improve • Gives career advice • Serves as a role model • Helps mentee learn to navigate corporate culture • Strives to increase mentee's sense of self-worth and job competence • Focuses on mentees' personal and professional development • Talks to their mentees face to face	• Must be senior leaders with influence • Tends to personally select who they will sponsor • Gives protégés exposure to other executives who could help their career • Makes sure their people are considered for promising opportunities and challenging assignments • Protects their protégés from negative publicity or damaging contact with senior executives • Advocates to get their people promoted • Talks about their protégés behind closed doors

to consider applying for an ERG leadership role. When executives describe the value of obtaining an advanced degree or certain type of certification (such as a Sig Sigma blackbelt), it widens the aperture through which an ERG member views their career trajectory. With such new perspectives gained from talent pipeline initiatives that focus on career planning advice gleaned by successful leaders, ERG members gain the confidence to take a more proactive approach toward their career planning. Plus, they learn that simply being smart and working hard will not automatically result in career advancement. A valuable perspective gained from such efforts is that ERG members realize that having ambition is an honorable intent, which ultimately encourages them to view their career progression as a worthy pursuit. This might be especially important for ERG members whose cultural background might frown upon an overt display of ambition.

Another common talent pipeline initiative undertaken by ERGs is helping their members bring their full selves to work and feeling that they can be their true authentic selves. ERGs focus on this topic because they understand that upward mobility may be difficult for members who feel they have to downplay or hide certain aspects of their identity to move ahead. When they do so, often called *covering,* others perceive this uncomfortableness and hesitancy as indicating that they lack confidence or that they are inauthentic. Such perceptions, whether accurate or not, may stall the promotional velocity of an ERG member.

To address this phenomenon, ERGs embark on a variety of talent pipeline approaches. For example, HOLA, the ERG for Google, periodically hosts a Latina leadership summit where they invite Latinas from the organization to gather, build their network, participate in professional development specifically geared for Latinas, and meet and connect with senior leaders within Google, thus raising their visibility. The Latino ERG at Facebook, called Latin@, holds a similar event called Latino Community Day and brings together hundreds of the Latino, Latina, and Latinx employees.

But the ultimate goal of both the HOLA and Latin@ organized events is to convey to their ERG members that their Hispanic heritage is an asset and a source of strength. They are encouraged to not only celebrate their heritage, but to embrace it as a key differentiator and as Latino superpower. Such events encourage Hispanic ERG members to highlight their bicultural background, emphasize their bilingual abilities, or showcase their global mindset, especially by those born and raised in Latin America. In today's more globalized world, such capabilities are at the very core of what it means to be an effective and inclusive employer.

In doing so, the employee resource groups at both Google and Facebook are helping to create a workplace environment that allows Hispanic employees to be their true authentic selves. This minimizes the necessity for their Hispanic employees to have to spend time and energy on hiding their heritage and thus reallocate that energy towards increased workplace performance. When ERG members feel that they can own their own personal sense of identity, and not have it defined by someone else, they feel more confident and it encourages them to be an authentic leader. And in doing so, such efforts by ERGs are supporting their organizations talent pipeline initiatives.

Instead of holding a similar internal Latino leadership or community summit, the Hispanic ERG for AbbVie, the biopharmaceutical company based in Illinois, allocates a significant portion of their Career pillar budget to pay the registration fee to send a large number of their ERG members to external leadership development programs designed specifically for Hispanic professionals. Such programs not only teach important leadership skills, but they also educate participants how their Hispanic heritage may influence how they show up as a leader. Such insights better prepare their Latino ERG members to understand when leaning into their Hispanic cultural script might be beneficial, as well as recognizing that certain Latino behavioral tendencies might not be as useful and should therefore be downplayed.

Of course, Hispanic ERGs like those at Google, Facebook, and AbbVie are not the only ERGs that hold similar affinity-based initiatives. Such programs are rising in popularity and prominence within all employee resource groups as a way to demonstrate that one's uniqueness can be leveraged as providing an advantage in today's more global and diverse society.

Some ERGs also put together talent summaries that highlight some of their ERG members. Such summaries are typically short, about half a page, and quickly review a member's work experience, key capabilities, educational background, significant accomplishments, and desired future roles within the organization. These summaries are then compiled and put into talent profile document that is then distributed strategically within the organization. The goal of such an initiative is to further elevate awareness of the top talent that exists within the ERG, which tends to be predominantly women and historically underrepresented minorities.

The Asian American ERG for an information technology company based in Dallas compiled such a talent profile book consisting of talent summaries of 50 of their Asian American ERG members. Whenever the ERG was made aware of internal job opportunities, not only were such openings shared with their ERG members, but the hiring manager was also sent a copy of the talent profile book by the ERG. In doing so, the ERG helped hiring managers consider talent they might have otherwise overlooked or not considered. The result of this talent pipeline initiative was increased visibility for Asian American ERG members and several members who were promoted or hired into new roles indicated that their talent summary was key in their initial consideration for the role. One hiring manager who selected one of the Asian American ERG members for a role in her department indicated that the talent profile she received conveyed that this particular employee had established a track record of sustained high performance across fundamentally different challenges. She mentioned that the key factor in the ERG member being selected over another candidate was that their sustained high performance across different, highly challenging scenarios provided insights into the candidate's resilience, ambition, and potential.

What the Career pillar ultimately does for the organization is to accelerate leadership capability and skill development for ERG members. In doing so, Career pillar initiatives ultimately fill a company's talent pipeline with employees who tend to have diverse backgrounds and inclusive leadership aptitude that is critical to the future success of the enterprise.

6 Community Pillar

Collaboration and External Outreach

Of the 4C pillars, Community is the one most likely to stir the soul and generate short-term wins for an ERG (See Figure 6.1). The year of 2020 brought feelings of uncertainty and anxiety unlike what many ERG members had ever known before. The coronavirus pandemic and subsequent sheltering in place put employees in unprecedented levels of isolation. While Zoom calls and Microsoft Teams webinars allowed us to remain social with coworkers, the same can't be said about the small daily interactions one has with one's fellow employees and broader community. The pandemic took away, at least for a while, those gala dinners supporting nonprofit fundraising events, a friendly chat with a colleague at the company cafeteria, or the social events commonly put on by employee resource groups.

Human beings are social creatures – we are naturally inclined to cooperate in order to not only survive but thrive. Science has proven that social distancing is an effective and necessary way to prevent the spread of coronavirus, but as the world reopens, ERGs are putting their pent-up communal energy toward reinvigorating their community efforts. Employee resource groups have come to understand that a sense of togetherness is a natural feeling when it comes to being human. This leads to a need for togetherness among people that is

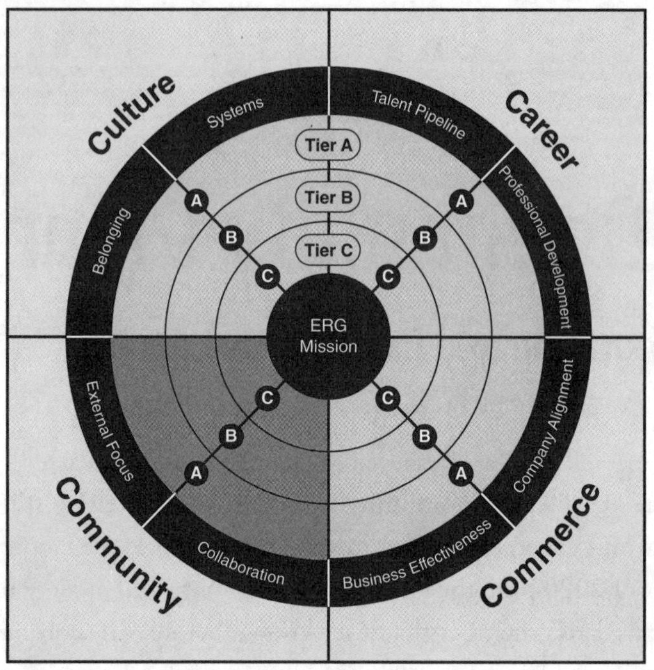

Figure 6.1 The Community 4C Pillar

fostered by strong community efforts often led by ERGs. When someone surrounds themselves with a support system of those in their community, it creates more opportunities to feel that warm, fuzzy feeling of belonging because we are acting in line with nature by coming together.

The impact of community initiatives by ERGs cannot be understated. By building a strong community with those having similar characteristics or of the same affinity, ERGs create more opportunities for their members. Big or small, a community can provide countless opportunities for ERG member growth and experience. By being a part of a community, the next time a member of an ERG needs to contact someone at work, it is likely there is someone in their community whom they can depend on to provide an introduction. When employees face a new diversity-related problem or challenge, ERG members can reach out to colleagues to find out if anyone has had an experience that could be valuable to them. With a community of fellow employees looking out for your best interests and working together to achieve the mission of the ERG, there is no shortage of support for opportunities to gain the communal feeling that members want.

Organizations also benefit from the external community initiatives of employee resource groups. For one, ERG community efforts help an organization to recognize and sympathize with the concerns of a specific community. ERG community efforts help to establish a relationship of trust and understanding between an organization and a community. Specific Community pillar initiatives by an ERG support a company in a variety of ways. For example, ERGs help with corporate image management. ERGs can help promote the desired perception of an organization in a specific community. As gay pride parades have grown across the country over the past decade, it is usually the LGBTQ ERG that helps to organize an organizations involvement in the parade via a float or group of employees representing the company. Such involvement helps to enhance an organization's name recognition and reputation within the gay community.

Most large organizations give charitable contributions to worthy nonprofit organizations to build good will. But often community affairs departments are challenged to channel limited funds designated by an organization for philanthropic purposes in the most impactful manner for both the community and the organization. ERGs, through their Community pillar initiatives, can thus help their organizations select the right nonprofit. For example, the Latino ERG for Google, HOLA, was instrumental in helping the organization select the Hispanic Heritage Foundation as a philanthropic partner. Google helps to fund the foundation's Code as a Second Language (CSL) program, which introduces Hispanic youth to computer programming. A key component of CSL is to supply students with an introductory skillset of web design and computer programming. The Hispanic community wins because it can fund a very important workforce development program for Latino youth. HOLA wins because they become a trusted advisor to Google regarding philanthropic causes. And Google wins because it is now helping to build the next generation of intellectual capital with skills that the company will need in the future.

Organizations at the local, state, and national levels offer an organization the opportunity to create and maintain relationships and support with influential contacts. Employee resource groups can thus help an organization's government and community affairs establish such relationships. General Electric, the American multinational conglomerate based in Boston, Massachusetts, has been an active supporter in the past of two key nonprofit, nonpartisan, social welfare, and public policy organizations – the Congressional Hispanic Caucus Institute (CHCI) and the Congressional Black Caucus Institute (CBCI). By supporting both the CHCI and CBCI, General Electric is helping to educate voters and train tomorrow's political leaders from both the Black and Hispanic communities. Both GE's Hispanic ERG and Black ERG help to support these two organizations via helping to identify scholarship recipients and internship participants. This demonstrates how ERGs can serve to help to community affairs and government affairs initiatives, an often-overlooked aspect of ERGs by organizations. Now that we have established that the Community pillar is important to ERGs, let's take a closer look at the two key ways they do so, external outreach and collaboration.

External Outreach and Focus

One of the many goals that ERGs tend to have is to give back to their external community. Whether it be through volunteering or fundraising, community outreach by ERGs helps give their members a sense of purpose. The feeling of giving back and contributing to society is unparalleled. Giving back is also a great way for ERG members to get to know their community. The volunteer efforts by ERGs are also very important to community organizations. Without volunteers, many services and events we enjoy in our communities would not be so readily available. When ERG members spend time helping a local shelter, participating in a backpack drive or supporting a food bank, they provide an important service to those less fortunate. I recall when Hurricane Maria devasted the island of Puerto Rico in September 2017. There was nothing so rewarding as to see the leaders of various Latino ERGs across the United States organize and collaborate to collect food, water, and clothing to send to the inhabitants of Puerto Rico. They filled truckloads of desperately needed supplies that we shipped to the island to help relieve the suffering and to help the survivors. Through their collective efforts, these ERGs accomplished more by working together than they could have had they each done a supplies drive on their own.

When ERGs help their members give back to the community, they support employee well-being in several ways. It is statistically proven that people who volunteer regularly are healthier both physically and mentally. Individuals who have volunteered throughout their lifetime typically live longer. Besides making employees healthier, volunteering helps them manage chronic health conditions, lower their stress, and have better psychological happiness. In addition to the health benefits, volunteering gives employees a sense of purpose. The fulfilling feeling of giving back and contributing to society is unparalleled. All these reasons provide the rationale as to why achieving ERG excellence requires that employee resource groups have community outreach initiatives such as volunteering.

Besides volunteering, ERGs at times raise scholarship funds. One of the best at this is the Latino ERG at AT&T called HACEMOS. Each year, HACEMOS raises hundreds of thousands of dollars through their ERG efforts. HACEMOS is allowed to raise scholarship funds because the ERG has established a scholarship foundation as a separate 501(c3) nonprofit organization. This distinguishes them from almost every other ERG in corporate America. Through various fundraising activities such as golf tournaments, dinners, and sales events, HACEMOS is deeply committed to raising scholarship funds that are ultimately given to bright Hispanic students. By doing so, not only is HACEMOS helping individual Hispanic students fund their education, but they are also seeding the pipeline of the next generation of upwardly mobile Latino professionals.

Along with volunteering, fundraising, and supporting nonprofits and community organizations, ERGs also serve in an advisory capacity for their organization with regard to which nonprofits to support. Human resources, community affairs, and diversity and inclusion functions oftentimes receive dozens of requests for support by community organizations and nonprofit groups. In many instances, ERGs can help in selecting which nonprofits an organization should support because of their deep knowledge of their community. For example, when the human resources department at The Home Depot, the home improvement retailer based in Atlanta, Georgia, was receiving many requests from organizations that support military veterans, they turned to their Veterans ERG for help. The members of the ERG who were military veterans were very familiar with most of the organizations requesting support. While these organizations each had a compelling mission of supporting veterans, some were more highly regarded than others by the veterans at The Home Depot. Leveraging the input and experience of their military veterans, The Home Depot determined which veteran nonprofits to support financially. Since these organizations had been selected with the input provided by their military veterans, The Home Depot was much more confident that they were indeed supporting organizations that were deemed worthy and credible by veterans. This is another example of how ERGs can support nonprofit organizations.

Employee resource groups can also help enhance the brand reputation of a company within a community. During the Black Lives Matter protests that occurred in 2020 due to the death of George Floyd, many companies put out statements that expressed grief, outrage, and sympathy about what had happened. Organizations took bold steps to convey their commitment to the Black community. They denounced systemic racism, they made pledges to support Black businesses and anti-racist organizations, and they made donations in support of Black organizations and historically Black colleges and universities. Some organizations even unveiled initiatives for addressing racism in their products or organizations.

In many instances, the Black ERGs at these organizations were solicited for input. They were asked for advice and helped in shaping some of these public proclamations of support for the Black community by organizations. But not only that, Black ERGs were often instrumental in sharing these internal actions with the broader Black community. Such actions helped to extend the impact of these efforts to support the Black community by raising awareness of those specific actions in hopes that other organizations will follow their lead. By raising awareness of specific actions taken by companies to support the Black Lives Matter movement, ERGs also helped their organizations to shift away from the approach some call "diversity pandering" and toward meaningful reform.

Collaboration Is Key

Because of their strong commitment toward building community, ERGs in many cases have become skilled at collaboration. There are many reasons ERGs make effective collaboration a key value. First, when ERGs collaborate, they learn from each other. They take an organizational approach towards learning from each other's successes and failures. When ERGs collaborate, they bring varied talents together, making of a pool of employees with different skills and knowledge. When more competent and experienced people are brought together, ERGs undergo better problem solving. And in today's increasingly polarized world, effective collaboration by ERGs improves the level of trust people have in each other. ERGs provide opportunities for members to regularly work together with people outside of their own team or department, and this is an effective way of building trust and is a necessary component of ERG excellence.

Collaboration among ERGs helps to eliminate silo mentality. The silo mentality crops up when ERGs fail to share important knowledge and information with each other. This can happen because an organization hasn't established the right systems or communication tools to let ERGs work together effectively, or it might happen because of active turf battles between ERGs that are super protective of information that they possess and do not wish to share.

Regardless of the reason, silo mentality within employee resource groups is dangerous and reduces the ability to achieve ERG excellence. For one, silo mentality lowers productivity by ERGs. When ERGs aren't aware of relevant information, or if they can't learn from the experience of other ERGs, they tend to be less productive. ERG resources also take a hit due to silo mentality. Whether it's redundant work, time spent searching for crucial information, or a duplication of similar ERG events, silos can result in the inefficient use of ERG funds. Jarring inconsistencies can also result when ERGs act in silos. When ERGs carry out their initiatives and activities in totally different ways, employees do not get a consistent experience when interacting with ERGs. This inconsistency can ultimately hurt the reputation and brands of ERGs.

Striving toward ERG excellence requires the elimination of silos and active collaboration. A simple solution for this is to establish a sort of governance council or steering committee consisting of the leaders of all the ERGs. When the ERG leaders gather, they can share information, provide updates, identify current challenges, share recent successes, and highlight upcoming initiatives and programs. In doing so, ERGs are facilitating information sharing and this can lead to more opportunities for collaboration. Recently I was invited to speak at one of these ERG steering committee meetings at an organization. Before my presentation, I sat as each ERG provided an update with the other ERG leaders. One particular ERG mentioned that they had identified a speaker to come speak to their group on the topic of personal branding and conveying executive presence. Several of the other ERGs then commented that they too had similar plans to address this topic in upcoming events. The ERGs ultimately agreed to partner and to have the external speaker give their presentation to all of ERGs, thus eliminating redundancy and saving resources as they agreed to share the cost of the speaker fee.

Striving for excellence also requires that ERGs benchmark with ERG at other companies. It amazes me as to why some ERGs do not do this more often, particularly given that similar ERGs often are trying to accomplish the same things, albeit at different companies. When ERGs benchmark, they gain a better perspective of how their ERGs stack up against others. The ultimate goal of benchmarking is continuous improvement, something all ERGs should aim for.

In my experience, ERGs tend to benchmark so that they can share best practices and so they can learn from each other. Connecting with ERGs at other companies can also lead to more collaboration opportunities. Benchmarking allows ERGs to make a bigger impact because they can learn from each other, have a larger impact, and share resources across organizations.

Sidebar: Consortium of Latino Employee Organizations (CLEO)

Allstate Corporation is an insurance company based in the northern Chicago suburb of Northbrook, Illinois. Because of its proximity to Chicago, many other corporations also have their headquarters or major offices in or near Northbrook, including Walgreen's, Baxter Healthcare, Astellas Pharma, CDW, Abbott Labs, AbbVie, Takeda, and Discover, to name a few. In 2008, the Latino ERG at Allstate realized that it was likely that many of these nearby companies also had Latino ERGs, and so they invited them to their headquarters to meet, share information, and explore ways to collaborate. Little did they know that this initial meeting would turn into the Consortium of Latino Employee Organizations (CLEO).

Today, CLEO is a national organization with three main chapters, CLEO Chicago, CLEO Twin Cities in Minneapolis/St. Paul, and CLEO Bay Area in Silicon Valley. Every quarter, each of the three CLEO chapters meets at the office location of a CLEO member company. When they meet, the host company provides an overview of their Latino ERG, then they have a speaker address a topic such as Latino talent acquisition or establishing ERG metrics, and then they have a networking event. Before the Covid-19 pandemic hit in 2020, the most recent CLEO quarterly meetings had been hosted by the Latino ERGs at Uber, Medtronic, Facebook, Twitter, Best Buy, US Bank, Google, Gilead Sciences, and Sony PlayStation, to name a few. Each meeting attracts about 60 to 80 Latino ERG members from a host of companies and has led to the sharing of numerous best practices, dozens of examples of collaboration, mutual learnings, and the collection of benchmarking data.

Cross-company ERG collaboration can also have other benefits, such as increased employee retention. The Latino population in the Twin Cities of Minnesota (Minneapolis/St. Paul) is still quite small, at about only 5 percent of the population. Thus, the larger employers in the Twin Cities often must recruit their Latino professionals outside of Minnesota from areas such as California, Texas, New York, or Florida. When these Latino professionals would move to Minnesota, many of the employers often found that they did not stay very long because they did not have roots in the local community. Prior to the formal establishment of CLEO, Isaias Zamarripa, who was the director of talent acquisition and diversity for General Mills at the time, started to bring together the Latino ERG leaders from top employers such as Best Buy, Target, 3M, and Land O'Lakes. But the purpose of the gatherings wasn't just so that the Latino ERGs could collaborate and benchmark; it was also to initiate the creation of a much larger professional Latino community in the Twin Cities. By connecting, the Latino professionals could share recommendations on top Latin restaurants, identify establishments that played Latin music, create friends to connect with outside of work, and find others from their home countries such as Venezuela, Peru, Colombia, and Mexico. By creating this network of Latino professionals, Isaias and the local employers were creating reasons for Latino professionals to stay in Minnesota. By helping these Latino professionals establish roots in the Twin Cities, these professionals did indeed stay longer, and companies saw an improved retention rate of their Latino and Latina professionals that were recruiting outside of Minnesota. This is an example of how the collaboration and community outreach efforts within the Community pillar of ERGs can help improve employee retention.

Besides collaboration by ERGs within the same company (intra-ERG) and between ERGs from various companies (Inter-ERG), employee resource groups can also collaborate with various departments and functional areas. When a large, multinational package delivery and supply chain company wanted to improve the inclusiveness of its talent management systems, it collaborated with its ERGs to find answers. Members of the various ERGs served as focus group participants and shared their experiences with the organizations talent management systems. Through these efforts, the company was able to identify three key insights. First, women and diverse professionals were often steered toward staff roles and not given roles with profit-and-loss responsibility. This ultimately hurt their chances of obtaining C-suite roles. Second, women and historically underrepresented ERG members described how they often felt that they had to repeatedly perform well in tough assignments before being promoted, while their white male colleagues seemed to be promoted simply based on their potential. And third, ERG members shared how they were often rated as "Not Ready Now" when it came time for promotions, while their nondiverse colleagues consistently were rated as "Ready Now" for promotions. By collaborating with the diversity and inclusion department and the talent management function, the ERGs were able to provide input that improved the company's talent management systems and were also able to broaden their influence and impact on the organization.

When ERGs have robust Community pillar initiatives, they demonstrate a unique ability to not only improve ERG member well-being and sense of purpose but also help to establish a communal spirit and extend the organizations' influence and reputation in the local, state, and national municipalities in which they operate.

7 Culture Pillar

Building a Culture of Excellence and Belonging

Of the 4C pillars, Culture is the one that can have the most impact on an organization. Culture is commonly defined as the set of shared attitudes, values, goals, and practices that characterizes an organization. In simpler terms, culture helps to define the proper way to think, act, and behave within an organization. Every company has its own unique culture and most indicate that they wish to foster a culture of inclusion in the workplace and thus want to eliminate feelings of "outsiderness" for any employee.

Yet even though companies wish to create an environment that is inclusive, many employees still feel like outsiders in the workplace. This causes them to further suppress the parts of themselves that make them distinctly unique from their coworkers. Feeling like an outsider is a personally painful and negative experience. The energy required to overcome feeling like an outsider at times can undermine one's focus and performance. The Culture pillar within the 4C Model™ helps companies fulfill their desire for inclusiveness by having individuality both noticed and valued. Workplace support, understanding, and trust all reduce the likelihood of an employee feeling like an outsider. That is why the impact of the Culture pillar can be so significant. The two segments that help to define the Culture pillar are Belonging and Systems (See Figure 7.1) and we will explore each.

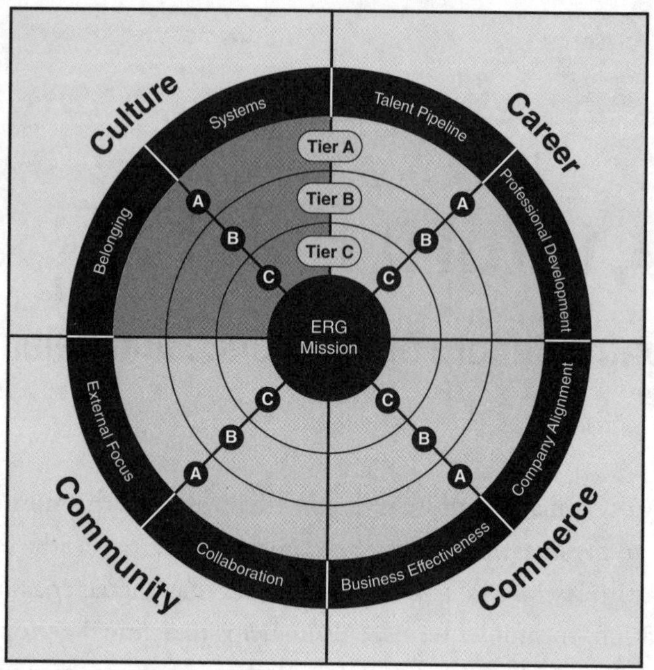

Figure 7.1 The Culture 4C Pillar

Belonging

When organizations talk about *diversity,* the use of the word is often linked to numbers and percentages that indicate a certain level of representation. Belonging "is about how you feel" when you are at work. "Do you feel valued? Do you feel like you should be there? Do you feel that your insights and opinions matter? Whereas diversity is focused on the organization, belonging is focused on the individual. Increasing employee sense of belonging can have numerous benefits. Some studies have found that workplace belonging can lead to an estimated 56 percent increase in job performance, a 50 percent reduction in turnover risk, and a 75 percent decrease in employee sick days. One study found that a single incident of feeling excluded by an employee can lead to an immediate 25 percent decline in an individual's workplace performance. ERG excellence requires that

ERGs leverage the Culture pillar to develop initiatives to help elevate the sense of belonging for employees.

Cultural celebrations are the most notable way in which employee resource groups elevate the sense of belonging. If a company is successful with their diversity initiatives, it usually results in having employees from varied backgrounds and cultures. Failing to recognize, embrace, and celebrate the diversity of a workforce does not promote inclusion. But when companies do celebrate diverse representation, employees feel their values, uniqueness, and heritage are fully appreciated. Since employee resource groups are usually formed by women and historically underrepresented groups, it is natural that they take a leadership role in cultural celebrations in the workplace.

Whether it be Black History Month in February, Women's History Month and Disability Awareness Month in March, Asian American Heritage Month and Military Awareness Month in May, Pride Month in June, or Hispanic Heritage Month in September, these are the moments when employee resource groups really shine. ERGs usually partner with their organization to have initiatives during these celebrations that highlight the culture, recognize leaders within the community, bring in speakers that note key contributions, promote increased awareness, hold panels with executives about the importance of a specific community, and generally promote various aspects related to a specific community or culture. Such efforts led by employee resource groups are highly effective at creating cultures of inclusion and help increase a sense of belonging by employees because these initiatives honor their unique contributions and convey that employees are accepted by and belong within the organization.

Another common Culture pillar initiative by employee resource groups that promotes belonging is one that encourages allyship. An ally is someone who is not a member of a particular underrepresented group but serves as a support and advocate. Allyship is increasingly championed by ERGs because it goes a long way toward building a sense of belonging. In fact, a growing trend by employee resource groups is to add the word *ally* to their name and thus they become the Women & Allies ERG, the Latinx & Allies ERG, the LGBTQ & Allies ERG, and so on. By doing so, ERGs are conveying that they welcome allies to become members of their group. By attracting more allies, ERG members gain a heightened sense of belonging. Allyship also promotes inclusion, because those who are not members of a historically underrepresented group do not feel excluded by employee resource groups. Therefore, men are encouraged to join the women's ERG. Heterosexuals are encouraged to join the LGBTQ employee resource groups, non-Hispanics are encouraged join the Latino ERG, and so on. This helps to convey the inclusiveness of employee resource groups and dismantles the argument that ERGs are exclusive.

Not only do employee resource groups welcome allies, but they also often help educate themselves and others on how to be an effective ally. For example, during Hispanic Heritage Month in 2020, the Latino ERGs from Uber, Zillow, CDW, Facebook, Medline Industries, Cox Enterprises, Genentech, US Bank, and Electronic Arts all invited me to be a guest speaker and discuss the importance of allyship. Each of these nine Latino ERGs wanted to educate attendees of what is an ally as well as the dos and don'ts regarding allyship. In doing so, these ERGs promoted belonging because they placed emphasis not just on the word *ally* as a noun (what is an ally?) but on *ally* as a verb (how does one convey allyship?).

Another Cultural pillar initiative by ERGs that promotes belonging is intersectionality. The word *intersectionality* is a legal term that was in relative obscurity outside of academic circles until 1989. It was then that professor Kimberlé Crenshaw used the word to describe how race, class, gender, and other individual characteristics "intersect" with one another and overlap. Because employee resource groups tend to focus on one aspect of an individual's identity, it is natural for ERGs to promote awareness of situations where the multiple dimensions of one's identity intersect.

Society is becoming more multicultural and multiethnic. As diversity and inclusion principles take hold, racial, ethnic, nationality, and gender relationship lines are becoming more fluid, and therefore easier to cross. Interracial couples have increased exponentially. Now their ethnically blended children are coming of age and defining their identities not as just black, or Latino, or Asian, but as Chinalatina, Blaxican, Mexipino, or Blackinese. This emerging demographic trend has significant implications for how organizations address their employee resource groups.

The US Census Bureau estimates that the country's mixed-race population tripled in size between 2010 and 2020. It also reported that by the year 2050, one in five US citizens would be multiracial. Current demographic statistics on multiracial individuals indicate they are already a larger population than Native Americans and Pacific Islanders. This multiracial movement is stronger among under-30 millennials who are more fluid and flexible on race and not as tradition-bound with rigid black and white categorizations. In addition, as members of the post–civil rights era, these younger Americans did not experience the same racially segregated world as previous generations did. Their new message is that they want their own identity to cross, rather than stop at, various demographic boundaries.

Diversity consultant Andrés Tapia reminds us that from a racial and ethnic perspective, the individuals refusing to be bucketed into just one category force us to rethink all demographic categories. Multiple identities are surfacing in other ways, too. Says Tapia, "As taboos against gays in the military fall away, we now meet not just the war veteran, but also the gayveteranXer. And, as women achieve parity in their overall representation in the workforce, it's not enough to talk just about women. We need to recognize the GenYlesbiansinglemother, the Boomerprofessionalwomanwithadultkids, or the singlewomanmuslimengineer." Pause for a moment and think about how today's ERGs are defined. Where do these emerging multidimensional-identity people fit? What ERG would they join?

ERG excellence calls for intersectionality to be considered crucial to the work of employee resource groups. Employee resource groups are calling for and participating in more dynamic conversations about the differences in experience among employees with multiple dimensions of overlapping identities. ERGs have led the way in increasing the level of awareness that without an intersectional lens, initiatives that aim to address exclusion and injustice towards one group may end up perpetuating systems of inequities towards other groups. In my opinion, the Women's ERGs were at the forefront of the intersectionality movement within employee resource groups. The reason being is that in most organizations, the women's employee resource group tends to have the most members, have the largest budget, receive the greatest amount of support, and have the highest percentage of senior leader participation.

But for a short while during their ERG evolution, the women's ERGs were often viewed as the "white women's" ERG because they lacked membership of women of color. Women from diverse racial and ethnic backgrounds often felt that the women's ERG did not address issues that most impacted women of color. But women ERGs quickly moved to eliminate this discrepancy and soon elevated the sense of urgency to address the issues to the most vulnerable members of their community. Before long, you started to see the women's ERG hold sessions on issues faced by Black women in the workplace, obstacles encountered by Latinas, the experience of lesbians in the LGBTQ community, and so on. Other ERGs soon followed in addressing their own challenges with intersectionality and thus started the movement where the Hispanic ERG would partner with the Black ERG to hold a session on what it is like to be Afro-Latino. The Disability ERG and the Military ERG started holding intersectionality events about the issues faced by veterans who become disabled because of their military combat experience. The working parents ERG would hold events with the LGBTQ employee resource group and hold a session on how to best show support for a child who is gay. I've been privileged to see all sorts of intersectionality events held by employee resource groups to further promote belonging. In doing so, employee resource groups emphasize that employees across these ERGs can become allies of each other.

When considering the future of diversity initiatives, this emerging multidimensional reality could significantly alter the current one-dimensional employee resource group landscape. In response, affinity groups should look out for the multidimensionality of identities within their own groups.

The Asian group can seek ways to address the unique challenges people with disabilities encounter within Asian cultures. Latino groups can bring to the surface the racial dimensions of being Afro Latino, Asian Latino, or Indigenous Latino. And this list could grow. We may begin to see more ERGs that acknowledge multiple identities, such as Gen Y women with children, Native Americans with disabilities, or multiracial gay men. These groups might spring up as subsets of already existing groups. For example, the women's network might form a discussion group for Gen Y women with children, and this group might dialogue with Baby Boomer women caring for elderly parents; or the LGBT network could establish a subgroup for multicultural gay employees.

As necessary as it is, this will not be an easy evolution, given how successful and entrenched the current ERG model can be. For companies just embarking on ERGs, this diversity of identities creates dilemmas about how they should begin.

I and other diversity consultants, such as Andrés Tapia, have been working with companies on addressing this issue. There has developed a cognitive understanding that multidimensional identities are an increasing reality; even so, our set ways of viewing ERG boundaries remain shaped by traditional thinking. There is also, understandably, a feeling of threat. In embracing multidimensionality there remains a risk of diluting a group's identity or purpose and of trying to be all things to all people and as a result being nothing to anyone. Embracing multidimensionality and intersectionality is a tall order and one that some ERGs would rather not face right now, given the many other challenges and opportunities in front of them. But denial won't make the issue of multidimensionality go away. And ERG excellence requires that employee resource groups tackle this issue head on if they wish to elevate the sense of belonging for all employees and all their multidimensionality and intersectionality.

Yet another way belonging is increased via the Cultural pillar is through initiatives that promote inclusive policies and employee benefits. Benefits applicable to all demographic groups, such as flexible work scheduling and emotional wellness programs, signal to employees that an organization cares about their distinct needs and demands inside and outside of work. Inclusive policies and benefits convey signs of appreciation that drive an increased sense of belonging. Thus, employee resource groups are helping their employers rethink their benefits so that they are applicable to a more diverse employee population. In return, employers are hoping that these positive changes put them on the path toward a more inclusive culture that further promotes a sense of belonging.

For example, the LGBTQ employee resource groups have been instrumental in changing company policies and benefits that now include domestic partners. Disability ERGs have been leaders in helping to make their workplace more accessible for employees who are visually impaired or in a wheelchair. Latino ERGs have helped their organizations to adopt policies that are more inclusive of immigrants or those born outside of the United States. Women's ERGs have pushed for benefits that cover childcare and eldercare expenses. Faith-based ERGs have helped to implement floating holidays so that employees of varying cultural and religious backgrounds can have days off for holidays that they wish. Male ally members of the women's ERGs have helped to get paid paternal leave for dads much like paid maternal leave for mothers. These are all examples of the benefits that can be attributed to the belonging initiatives of an employee resource group.

In 2017, Uber, the ride-hailing and food delivery company based in San Francisco, conducted a thorough audit of its compensation strategy and made adjustments to reflect the market and close the pay gap between men and women. Around the same time, Uber's Black and Hispanic ERGs partnered to promote pay equity for engineers of color, resulting in similar salary adjustments. Ultimately, Uber launched the Racial Equity Leadership Council (RELC) to ensure accountability and serve as the body responsible for operationalizing Uber's commitments to building racial equity internally and externally. RELC is composed of senior leaders across Uber's business units and geographies. More importantly, the council consists of ERG leaders from Asian at Uber, Black at Uber and Los Ubers employee resource groups. The result is that ERG leaders at Uber are helping the company meet their racial equity commitments, which further promotes employee belonging.

An additional way that belonging has been manifested via the Culture pillar of employee resource groups is through support of diversity recruiting initiatives. Such initiatives help to convey the inclusive nature of an organization at the very beginning of the employee life cycle. Not only do employee resource groups help an organization recruit from a more diverse talent pool, but they also help to ensure that they have culturally competent hiring practices. For example, the People with Different Abilities, Caregivers and Family Members (ADAPT) ERG at Catalent Pharma Solutions worked with the recruiting department and the marketing department to create a short five-minute animated video that serves as a resource for hiring managers who are interviewing candidates with a disability. Video describes what to do should a candidate arrive to an interview with a service animal, or how to approach a candidate who is visually impaired. Also outlined in the video are insights regarding providing workplace accommodations to candidates needing them. With such a video, the ADAPT employee resource group helps Catalent extend a sense of belonging even to job candidates. Similarly, the Latino ERG at BNY Mellon held a workshop with the talent acquisition department that highlighted differences that might appear during the interview process of Hispanic candidates. They outlined how Hispanic heritage could result in candidates answering questions in a manner different than what a hiring manager might expect. While being careful not to promote stereotypes, the Latino ERG did want to highlight common Latino archetypes based on behavioral tendencies. An example of this is how the ERG described how Hispanics tend to be more collectivist in nature. This means that when Hispanics describe their work accomplishments, they are more likely to describe such things as team accomplishments versus individual accomplishments and they are likely to use the word *we* as opposed to *I*. For a hiring manager who is not culturally competent, they may interpret this as the Hispanic candidate not having individual accomplishments to talk about and thus rate them poorly in the interview. By sharing this and other Hispanic behavioral tendencies, the Latino ERG is promoting belonging through more inclusive hiring practices.

Having a sense of belonging is a common experience. Belonging means acceptance as an employee within an organization. A sense of belonging is a human need, just like the need for food and shelter. Feeling that you belong is most important in seeing value in your place within a company and that you are relevant, especially groups of employees who have been marginalized and underrepresented. ERG efforts that encourage inclusion and belonging help to make everyone responsible for achieving D&I goals day-to-day. The Culture pillar activities of ERGs encourage employees to value what each person can bring to the workplace by caring for one another, advocating for everyone's voice to be heard, and investing in their colleagues' growth and development. ERGs thus incorporate employee input into organizational values to show individuals they have a meaningful, equitable role in building a more inclusive workplace.

ERG efforts to promote inclusion and belonging help to prevent cultural destructiveness, which means that some employees refuse to acknowledge the presence or importance of cultural differences. This disregard for diverse cultures may be seen in workplace behaviors or policies that are damaging to certain cultures and to individuals living within that culture.

ERGs also help to prevent cultural incapacity, which refers to a view in which cultural differences are ignored. In the workplace, this may surface in the form of an overly narrow view of what leaders should look like or how they should act, without consideration of cultural factors that may be relevant to an overall understanding of an individual's strengths.

The Culture pillar of employee resource groups also helps to prevent cultural blindness, which involves an active belief that cultural differences are of no importance. Cultural differences may be noted, but being colorblind and culture-blind is considered a desired state. For example, companies often teach that their performance management systems are based on a system of meritocracy and that promotions are based solely on individual merit. In a meritocracy, a fair and equitable work environment creates a competitive system. Those who outperform their peers get promoted. In a meritocracy, hard work pays off, and each person, judged solely on results, rises to the fullness of their potential.

Proponents of a meritocracy say the issue of race, ethnicity, and gender do not matter because merit is all about performance. However, if a meritocracy is in place within most organizations, how do we explain the shortage of women and people of color in top corporate roles? What can be holding our organizations back from delivering on the promise and the values of the intended outcomes of a meritocracy?

Culture pillar initiatives by ERGs create a cultural competency within an organization that encourages recognition and responsiveness to cultural differences along with efforts to address systemic problems through advocacy. ERG Culture pillar initiatives related to belonging promote open acknowledgment of the need for cultural competency and active pursuit of holding cultural competence and proficiency in high regard.

Systems

Up to this point, we have not touched on the importance of ERG governance systems and operating practices. Without solid ERG infrastructure, achieving excellence will be nearly impossible. ERG operating guidelines, organizational structure, and governance practices provide the very foundation that ERG excellence can be built upon. Focusing on governance systems and practices may not sound exciting or glamourous, but it is essential if an ERG wants to perform with distinction. From my perspective, ERG governance systems are an attempt to create a culture of excellence within an employee resource group. That is why systems initiatives are placed within the Culture pillar of the 4C Model.

I've seen hundreds of ERG playbooks, handbooks, and policy manuals. Most are rather boilerplate and outline key aspects of effective employee resource group operations. Such manuals often define what an employee resource group is, what it is not, steps to forming an ERG, common roles, and various operational aspects as such as bylaws, compliance with company policy, and establishing an ERG charter. Such policies are often drafted by the office of diversity and inclusion with support from human resources.

But ERG excellence is not about following playbooks and procedures. ERGs indeed must follow company protocol, but avoiding mediocrity requires more than playing by the rules. Excellence demands that ERGs have measurement systems in place, have a high-performing ERG leadership team in place, a structure that works at both a global and local level and that there is a regular cadence to ERG activities. Let's explore these individually.

Measurement Strategy

Having a measurement strategy allows ERGs to measure their impact and should inform their decisions. At its core, an ERG measurement strategy is an all-encompassing plan that establishes how ERG goals will be measured. An ERG measurement strategy usually follows a path beginning with top-line ERG objectives, which are then broken down into measurable goals or metrics. A robust ERG measurement strategy will create clear communication across all the ERG stakeholders. This ensures everyone within an ERG is operating against the same objectives and goals. Finally, a measurement strategy helps to define what success looks like for an employee resource group. An ERG's measurement strategy falls under their systems initiatives. Measurement is so critical to the success of ERGs that Chapter 10 of this book is dedicated solely to ERG metrics and measurements.

High-Performing Leadership Teams

Employee resource groups also need systems in place that will promote the establishment of an effective ERG leadership team. An ERG's leadership team usually consists of the ERG chair or co-chairs, committee leads, chapter leaders, and other ERG members in key governance roles. In my experience, ERGs don't spend nearly enough time on systems that ensure leadership team effectiveness. Those that do tend to focus on the following initiatives. First, high-performing ERG leadership teams focus on how they will work together. This means they are intentional in determining how the team will work together and focus on becoming a well-oiled ERG leadership machine whose plans are carefully orchestrated team efforts. These teams realize that members cannot contribute if they do not know what is expected of them. Therefore high-performing leadership teams must focus on clarity, precision, and attention to detail. These leadership teams realize that even good intentions and a great effort won't get the ERG very far if they are doing the wrong things or doing the right things incorrectly. For example, I recall attending an offsite leadership team meeting for an employee resource group for an oil and gas company. Part of the retreat involved studying how NASCAR pit crews and surgery operation teams work together effectively even in high-pressure situations.

High-performing ERG leadership teams also are effective at conflict resolution. They acknowledge that conflicts can arise, and they realize that they can't have a high-performing ERG leadership team if they are not able to address tough issues head on. They also have the belief that some conflict might help the ERG leadership team come up with better solutions. Granted, ERG leadership team harmony is nice and desired, but not at the expense of leadership team effectiveness. During leadership team meetings, they are not afraid to air out ERG team issues and work to resolve them immediately. These teams understand that it is best to keep tough issues on the table until resolved. If they brush them under the rug, these teams know the issue will only fester and will hurt their leadership team performance (see Chapter 2 on ERG Derailers). In helping to create high-performing ERG leadership teams, the ERG leaders at Allstate Insurance Company usually participate in conflict management courses together.

Another characteristic of a high-performing ERG leadership team is that they constantly self-monitor and self-correct. These teams take time to consistently appraise how the team is doing and working together. They reflect and debrief often, especially after key ERG initiatives and events. They are not afraid to ask, "What's getting in the way of our high performance?" or "What needs to happen so that we perform better next time?" High-performing ERG leadership teams need to be able to handle the stress associated with self-analysis and must be able to call attention to dysfunctional team processes. This analysis can lead to situations that can get tense, but no more so if the ERG leadership team is not performing.

High-performing ERG leadership teams take the time to recognize and reward each other. They make sure to pay attention to each other. They support and nurture each other and don't hesitate to show approval and take the time to simply bond. A common characteristic that appears among high-performing ERG leadership teams I've worked with is that they are quick to offer words of encouragement to each other, they send notes of appreciation, they enjoy shared cups of coffee, and they give each other sincere gratitude. They even share awards with each other. I recall being invited to an ERG leadership team recognition dinner and they gave out a prize to the recipient of the "Turtle Award," which was given to the ERG leadership team member who wasn't afraid to stick their neck out to try something new. These high-performing ERG leadership teams realize the importance of showing gratitude, acceptance, and approval for each other.

Consistent Operating Rhythm

Another characteristic of employee resource groups that have strong governance systems in place is that they tend to be able to establish a consistent operating rhythm and cadence to their ERG initiatives. The *Oxford Dictionary* definition of rhythm is a "strong, regular, repeated pattern of movement or sound." When operating rhythm is applied to an ERG, it means a strong, regular, repeated pattern of employee resource group initiatives and events. Similarly, operating cadence is the pace at which ERG work is done and organized. When an ERG can establish both a regular operating rhythm and cadence, it tends to lead to a sense of forward-moving momentum that ERG members appreciate. It helps to keep ERG work moving along and typically leads to predictable results.

This consistency helps to bring order to the employee resource group and tends to improve ERG performance. Consistency also helps to establish a positive reputation for an ERG because it tends to lead to a track record of success. Employee resource groups that strive for excellence understand that a consistent operating rhythm is about ensuring that certain vital activities are performed in a consistent manner to a high degree of excellence with the purpose of driving efficiency, effectiveness, and therefore productivity. Some of the employee resource groups at General Electric have excelled at establishing a consistent operating rhythm and cadence. For example, at a recent CLEO Chicago event hosted by GE, their Hispanic employee resource group, called the GE Hispanic Forum, shared the operating cadence and rhythm for their events via their calendar of events. The calendar is reproduced in Table 7.1. A review of the calendar shows incredible

Table 7.1 GE Hispanic Forum – Chicago Hub Calendar ERG Meeting Cadence & Operating Rhythm

Hispanic Forum ERG Calendar	Q1			Q2			Q3			Q4		
	J	F	M	A	M	J	J	A	S	O	N	D
ERG meeting	•	•	•	•	•	•	•	•	•	•	•	•
Budget review			•			•			•			•
Volunteer day						•						•
Member workshop		•		•		•		•		•		•
Exec. sponsor mtg.												
Metrics review	•			•			•			•		
Culture event									•	•		
Lead team meeting	•		•		•		•		•		•	
Lunch event				•						•		
Committee meeting		•		•		•		•		•		•
Commerce event			•			•			•			•

consistency in meeting regularity that is appreciated by all the ERG stakeholders. GE Hispanic Forum members can also plan their level of participation based on their own schedules, being more active when their job allows for extra flexibility and participating less when work demands are high. In addition, when ERG members see the variety of different events and meetings, it allows them to get involved in ways that appeal to their interest and availability.

Organization Structure

The final component of effective ERG governance systems is their organization structure. The org structure of an employee resource tends to vary due to a variety of factors such as the size of the ERG, number of chapters, ERG roles, whether governance is centralized or decentralized, and if the ERG has a global presence. In all my experience with employee resource groups, I have yet to find a single best approach with regards to optimal ERG organization structure. There are simply too many variables to take into consideration.

However, there are two aspects related to organization structure that tend to promote ERG excellence. They are consistency and scalability. By consistency, I mean that each of the ERGs within a single organization has a relatively similar ERG organizational structure. For example, I once worked with a client organization whose ERG organization structures were all over the place. Their Women's ERG had two co-chairs. Their Veterans and LGBTQ ERGs each had a single leader they called a president. The Hispanic ERG also had a single leader but was not called a president but rather the global lead. And their disability ERG did not have a single leader but rather a governance council consisting of seven individuals who made up their leadership team. When I connected with the D&I executive at the company, they indicated that each ERG could determine their own organization structure based on what they considered would work best for them. The D&I executive admitted that while it sounded like a great idea at the time and each ERG supported this approach, the lack of consistency was leading to huge problems.

The inconsistent org structures made it difficult to apply ERG policies and procedures that applied to each. This caused dissension and confusion. Collaboration among the ERGs was challenging because each had to get different levels of approval before proceeding. Communication among the ERGs was difficult and common goals were more difficult to identify. Resentment also rose as some ERGs felt others were being treated more favorably based on their organization structure.

This is a classic example of why ERG excellence calls for consistency across employee resource groups within the same company. It does not matter if the ERG organization structure is more centralized or decentralized; what matters is the consistency across the groups. The consistency helps to promote collaboration, eases communication, results in reliable application of policies, reduces confusion and resentment, and ultimately helps to promote similar goals across each of the employee resource groups.

The second aspect related to ERG organization structure is scalability. While an organization does want consistency across their employee resource groups, the size and scope of each may vary. That is why I am not advocating for the same org structure across the ERGs, but rather, a similar organization structure that allows for scalability. With regards to ERGs, scalability refers to the capacity of the organization structure to change in size or scale. For employee resource groups to have scalable organization structures, they must each have a solid foundation. This foundation thus provides a platform for future ERG growth.

I am often approached by organizations that plan to launch employee resource groups, and they desire my help in making sure their ERGs are started properly. One of the first areas I advocate for is the establishment of a scalable ERG organization structure. The first step is to develop various tiers for their employee resource groups. I usually recommend the establishment of three tiers. Each tier has a set of characteristics and thresholds that must be met before the ERG is considered to have evolved to the next tier. Once the tier is established, a corresponding ERG organization structure is proposed for each tier. However, the ERG structures are scalable so that as the employee resource group grows, additional roles are added to the ERG organizational structure. The result is that each ERG has the same organization structure, which not only provides the solid foundation, but also allows for scalability. Table 7.2 outlines the characteristics and thresholds of the three tiers that I often recommend to companies launching ERGs.

Table 7.3 outlines the corresponding organization structure that matches each one of the three tiers.

Another component tied to organization structure and scalability is an employee resource group's capability to expand effectively via national or global chapters. There are many key considerations an employee resource group must undertake before deciding to launch additional chapters. These considerations are summarized in Table 7.4. Employee resource groups should conduct serious deliberations before adding field chapters. While additional chapters do allow an employee resource group to attract more members and grow their influence, if the conditions are not favorable for a new chapter at a specific location or in a specific country, it reduces the probably of a successful chapter launch experience. Each of the items in Table 7.4 should be analyzed and discussed within the ERG leadership team, the executive sponsor, and diversity and inclusion before initiating a new chapter. The greater the number of things in place to support a successful launch, the more positive the chapter launch experience will be for everyone.

This chapter has outlined the tremendous impact that employee resource groups can have via their Culture pillar initiatives. Not only

Table 7.2 Three-Tier ERG System: Tier Characteristics and Thresholds

ERG Characteristic and Tier Threshold	Tier 1 ERG Building Stage	Tier 2 ERG Intermediate Stage	Tier 3 ERG Advanced Stage
Minimum of 10 members	•	•	•
Underrepresented group	•	•	•
ERG leader identified	•	•	•
4C Model adopted	•	•	•
Executive sponsor identified	•	•	•
Hold at least four successful events	•	•	•
Business plan developed	•	•	•
ERG strategy clearly defined	•	•	•
Between 75 and 200 members		•	•
Successfully held ERG events		•	•
Effective use of ERG funds		•	•
Has regular meeting cadence		•	•
Career, Community, & Culture events		•	•
Strong leadership continuity		•	•
Impact on business goals / initiatives			•
201 + members			•
ERG metrics and scorecard in place			•
Address all 4Cs successfully			•
Strong leadership team in place			•
Capable of overseeing field chapters			•

Table 7.3 Three-Tier ERG System: Scalable Organization Structure Roles by Tier

ERG Organization Structure Roles	Tier 1 ERG Building Stage	Tier 2 ERG Intermediate Stage	Tier 3 ERG Advanced Stage
Office of Diversity and Inclusion	•	•	•
Executive sponsor	•	•	•
National ERG president	•	•	•
National ERG vice president	•	•	•
Community Committee lead	•	•	•
Culture Committee lead	•	•	•
Membership Committee lead	•	•	•
Career Committee lead		•	•
Communication Committee lead		•	•
ERG chapter president			•
ERG chapter vice president			•
ERG chapter Community Committee lead			•
ERG chapter Culture Committee lead			•
ERG chapter Membership Committee lead			•
ERG chapter Career Committee lead			•
ERG chapter Communication Committee lead			•

Table 7.4 Effective ERG Expansion: National or Global Chapters

Key Considerations	Established
Overall ERG strategy and focus is clearly defined	✓
Strong history of successful execution of ERG events and initiatives	
Governance / leadership policies established	✓
Expansion support from D&I, executive sponsor, & ERG membership	✓
Clear understanding of how company operates differently in field / global locations	
Strong knowledge of how ERG member profile may be different in field / global locations	
Understanding of funding and budget allocation for field / global location	✓
Healthy and collaborative relationship with D&I, HR, and internal stakeholders	✓
Established thresholds that must be met before an ERG chapter can be launched	
Demonstrated support / endorsement from field / global leadership	
Operation guidelines for chapter launch in place	
Decision made if field / global chapters will run as separate entities or if they are an "extension" of the home office ERG	

can ERGs help to enhance employee belonging through a variety of initiatives, but their ability to establish a culture of excellence through their governance systems allows them to do so. Thus, the Culture pillar within the 4C Model can impact an entire organization, and ERGs should leverage this pillar effectively as they strive for ERG excellence.

8 Commerce Pillar

No Longer an Underutilized Business Asset

The primary goal of the Associate Resource Group (ARG) Leadership Summit was to recharter the company's network groups as active change agents focused on business impact. The chief diversity officer (CDO) at Avon Products, a personal care organization based in New York, had convened the leaders of the company's ARGs to challenge them to create plans in line with this goal. The CDO was concerned that these groups were at risk of being viewed only as social networks. During the meeting, the ARG leaders and CDO discussed Avon's recent business results, which were not satisfactory. Avon's CEO at the time joined the two-day meeting to reinforce the importance of these groups and to invite ARG leaders to develop plans that support Avon's business strategies.

The ARG leaders rose to the occasion and immediately began work on refining and enhancing their plans. As an example, AHORA, Avon's Latino ARG, established plans to partner with Avon's southwest sales management teams to provide education and greater understanding of Latino culture and consumer behaviors. The group compiled and shared detailed market data for selected sales territories primarily serving Latino representatives and customers. The project also included the establishment of quantitative metrics, which allow all to understand how this effort has led to increased sales. AHORA is now well positioned and welcomed as an influential resource by the company's US sales leadership team. Additionally, AHORA partnered with the leader of Avon's Hispanic Market Initiatives to drive the business case and plans for Avon's Hispanic market outreach.

Similarly, Avon's Pride Network has sponsored and leveraged the use of product sampling and couponing at external LGBT events, like Pride Celebrations, parades, and other events to profile and share Avon products with this influential consumer segment. The Pride leaders invite Avon sales representatives to these events, which has directly resulted in new customers and sales.

The initial reactions have been very positive. US leadership teams have endorsed and welcomed the ARG's active involvement. More importantly, Avon's ARGs are alleviating the social network stigma and improving their internal reputations as resource groups capable of having tremendous impact on Avon's business, just as the CDO had challenged them to do.

Today, the notion that ERGs are just social circles still lingers in many other firms. Until these groups make a more deliberate effort to help drive deep business results, this outdated view will prevent ERGs from receiving the true credit they deserve. This stigma creates a lack of ERG credibility that leads to limited budgets, lukewarm support of employees' ERG involvement, and the damning faint praise of ERGs being a nice "diversity" program.

Some companies believe a simple name change from employee resource group (ERG) to business resource group (BRG) is enough to alter its reputation. However, it takes more to ensure that employee networks make a business impact. Other companies believe that forming a commerce or business impact committee will bring positive change. While well intentioned, neither approach creates the systematic or structural changes necessary to truly help an ERG become better aligned with business results.

ERGs derive power from the broad range of perspectives contributed by their members. Unfortunately, many organizations haven't embraced this diversity in their Commerce initiatives (See Figure 8.1). Their ERGs have failed to draw out the vitality and potency of their members' stories, dreams, and wishes from a Commerce perspective. As a result, members' ideas are not brought to the surface and ERGs are unable to support revenue generation or cost containment initiatives.

Without bold steps to improve ERGs' impact on Commerce efforts, the very existence of ERGs is threatened.

Next-generation ERGs make the biggest business impact by focusing on two areas: consumer insights and market penetration, both which help to expand the customer base. From a consumer insights perspective, ERGs should strive to serve as internal advisors for their firm's sales and marketing departments on how to reach unique markets. Because of their natural understanding of diverse

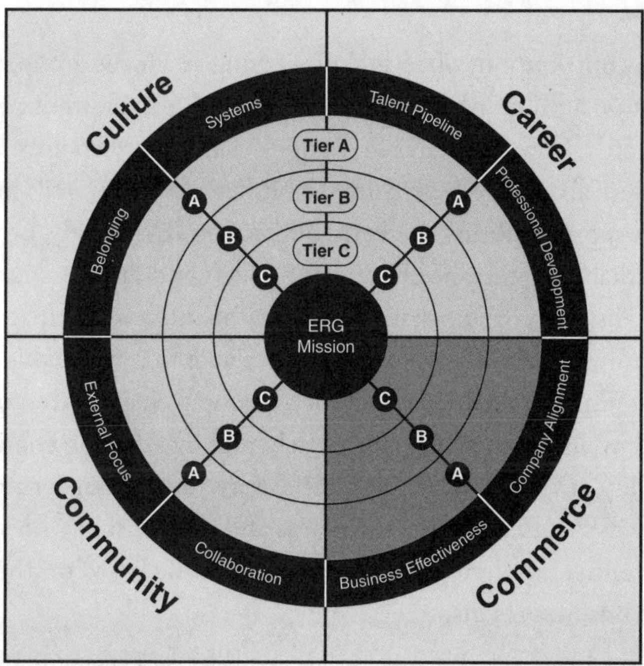

Figure 8.1 The Commerce 4C pillar.

market segments, ERGs are well positioned to provide unique cultural insights, establish relationships with community leaders, and build trust among these consumers.

Recently, a chief diversity officer for a Minneapolis-based company gave a presentation at the Multicultural Forum on Workplace Diversity. During her talk, she described the highly insightful diverse consumer perspectives the company's ERGs were providing. She spoke of how the African American network was offering input on how their automotive industry products could better appeal to Black millennials. The military ERG was instrumental in identifying US military market opportunities, and Asian ERG leaders were making introductions for top company leaders in various Chinese markets to drive business development relationships. Similarly, the Latino ERG presented unique insights to encourage Latinos to provide product reviews for the company's emarketplace initiatives. The ERGs at the company epitomize the new generation of ERGs and their focus on commerce initiatives.

ERG contributions often include serving as a focus group, providing input on affinity marketing initiatives, and testing products prior to launch to ensure they cater to unique customer preferences. Some of the most advanced ERGs actually establish advisory councils in which members support affinity marketing initiatives. Ultimately, firms see the remarkable significance in capturing likes and dislikes straight from the distinct consumer segments they are hoping to tap. Sometimes the only internal corporate resource able to provide this is an ERG. What a valuable market focus group to have within one's corporate walls. With such an approach, and by affecting company profitability, it's no wonder these ERGs serve as an asset for the company. ERGs that achieve this status and relationship with various business units can often justify increased funding based on their achieved business results.

ERGs must also be leveraged to strengthen and sustain a brand's status in diverse consumer segments. My belief is that ERGs should be challenged to bring forth those very profound consumer insights that a conventional product leader typically pays a lot of money to obtain.

Firms that do this successfully do so by highlighting the uniqueness that their members bring to the organization.

These organizations have figured out that true innovation and creativity is best achieved by inviting ERGs, and their diverse perspectives, to contribute to the idea-generation process.

It's an approach that makes sense, especially given the consumer buying power of various market segments, including a burgeoning racial and ethnic minority market in the US that is in the trillions of dollars. In response, then, we see the Asian ERG at Columbus, Ohio-based Nationwide Insurance helping educate the city's Asian community about the company's insurance products. At Clorox, the African American and Latino ERGs sponsor events that showcase Clorox's Kingsford BBQ charcoal. The various ERGs at Eli Lilly provide the company with insights on perceptions of diabetes. In turn, those insights are embedded into culturally relevant education outreach programs on the treatment of diabetes. And at John Deere, the African American ERG played a key role in making connections to the National Conference of Black mayors that over the years has led to millions of dollars' worth of landscaping equipment sales to municipalities. More and more next-generation ERGs are working on a value proposition that includes helping their companies on multicultural marketplace outreach.

I begin this Commerce chapter with positive examples to convey that despite ERG successes in driving business results, ERGs often still do not get the credibility and respect that they deserve, particularly from middle managers. Those who are not members of an ERG likely have perceptions of what an ERG does that are not accurate. Others have a sense of the initiatives that ERGs undertake, but still lack a thorough understand of the value an ERG provides. Without this comprehensive understanding, non-ERG members possess awareness that is incomplete. This lack of solid comprehension is bound to lower the standings of an ERG.

But for middle managers, my experience finds that there are two reasons they often do not support ERGs strongly. First, they feel that if their employees are participating in ERG activities, that is time and energy that the employee is not dedicating to helping meet the goals of their department or function. They simply do not like the idea of having their direct reports using company time to participate in these "non-work essential" activities. Therefore, they tend to discourage participation in ERGs, resent those employees that do, or even consider lowering the employee's performance rating because of their perceived lack of dedication to their "day job."

Other middle managers see employee resource groups as either being divisive or just a waste of time. They simply do not see the value that ERGs provide an organization. These managers still have the image of ERGs as being the "food, flag, and fun" folks whose social activities waste company resources. And because of these feelings, they tend to marginalize ERG activities and employees who support ERGs. Even when corporate executives champion ERGs and cite their contributions, these middle managers tend to be unmoved. The Commerce pillar within the 4C Model provides ERGs the ability to not only impact the bottom line, but also garner the credibility and respect within an organization that ERGs deserve. But to do so, ERGs must master the two segments that fall within the Commerce pillar: organizational alignment and business effectiveness.

Organizational Alignment

For an ERG to have robust Commerce pillar initiatives, they must align their initiatives with that of the organization. Every organization has a strategic plan that outlines where it is going and how it intends to get their while managing the changes that lie ahead. Often these strategic plans outline key initiatives that the company will pursue to meet their objectives. ERGs must have alignment so that they can connect their efforts with the organization's overarching strategic goals, objectives, and actions. Alignment allows ERG members to have line of sight of the enterprise strategy and informs how the actions of the ERG matter in the overall strategic picture. Alignment occurs when ERGs are synchronized and thus make decisions, act, and allocate ERG resources that is consistent with the overall organizational strategy.

Gradually, organizational alignment begins showing up in ERG plans, initiatives, and events. Strategic alignment can have an influence in every ERG activity and should become an integral part of ERG success. Without strategic alignment, ERG members become confused about their priorities, make fewer effective decisions, and this likely leads to more conflict. This also eventually leads to fatigue and causes employees to lose their passion and motivation as ERG members. Lacking organizational alignment, well-meaning ERG leaders may spend countless hours pursuing initiatives that, while they may be good initiatives, are not the right things to focus on at the time. This ultimately lowers the standing of ERGs and leads to cynicism about their overall contributions to an organization.

Want to know if your ERG has strategic alignment with organizational goals? Consider these two questions. First, how does your ERG support fulfillment of your company's purpose? Purpose is what the business is trying to achieve. Strategy is how the business will achieve it. Purpose is enduring – it is the north star toward which the ERG should point. Strategy involves choices the ERG makes regarding initiatives to pursue, values to hold, and members to attract. Leaders should look at their ERG and ask, "How well does our ERG support the fulfillment of our company purpose?" If your ERG is unclear about your company's strategic priorities, or its purpose, then it is likely the ERG is not strategically aligned. Next ask, "How well does our ERG support the achievement of our organizational strategy?" To maintain strategic alignment, an ERG must flex and change as business strategy itself shifts. If your ERG is incapable of helping the company execute its strategy, the strategy itself is diluted and the company's purpose will have to be fulfilled without the support of employee resource groups. For these reasons, ERG systems must align with the overall goals of the organization. Employee resource groups can promote organizational alignment through a variety of initiatives that we will explore here.

Executive Sponsors

My good friend Jennifer Brown, founder and CEO of Jennifer Brown Consulting, once conducted some amazing research on executive sponsors for ERGs. Her research led to the identification of five key roles that executive sponsors play. Those roles are strategist, broker, mentor, evangelist, and innovator. In my opinion, of these five roles, the strategist and broker roles help the ERG the most with organizational alignment. According to Jennifer Brown's research, when playing the strategist role, an executive sponsor helps an ERG align their initiatives with organizational goals. Their role is to help elevate ERG discussion and initiatives so that they support the attainment of key goals. They accomplish this by sharing business priorities with ERGs and then help the ERG shape initiatives that support these goals. Jennifer Brown also highlights that executive sponsors advocate for the ERGs position on signature issues. This often enables an ERG to become involved in key issues that impact an organization.

For example, I was invited to participate in a summit hosted by Comcast Corporation, the telecommunications company headquartered in Philadelphia. This summit was taking place in Denver, CO, and included the leaders of their ERGs that worked out of their West region. One of the speakers at the summit served as an executive sponsor for one of the ERGs. He highlighted how one of the company's strategic priorities in the West region was to lower the turnover rate for employees working in their call centers. The turnover rate was proving to be expensive for the organization due to the hiring and training cost involved with replacing employees who left the organization. While the turnover rate was low by industry standards, Comcast saw a competitive advantage if it could improve employee retention in its call centers.

By sharing this information with the ERG leaders, this executive sponsor was inviting them to align some of their ERG initiatives to this organizational goal. The ERGs were quick to respond. They held a brainstorming session on how ERGs could improve call center employee retention and identified initiatives they could launch. Within 18 months of this summit meeting, Comcast had drastically improved call center employee retention, and part of the success was attributed to initiatives launched and supported by their ERGs. This helped to elevate ERG credibility and company standing in Comcast's West region.

The broker role outlined by Jennifer Brown also helps an ERG establish organizational alignment. Based on Jennifer Brown's research, executive sponsors serve as brokers when they leverage their influence to provide ERG access to influential leaders and make introductions on behalf of an ERG to important people both inside and outside the organization. In essence, the broker role allows an executive sponsor to leverage their clout to advance ERG endeavors.

Stanley Black & Decker, Inc., based in New Britain, Connecticut, is a Fortune 500 American manufacturer of industrial tools and household hardware and provider of security solutions. One of the company's businesses is providing commercial electronic security and access solutions to hospitals, schools, retailers, airports, and academic institutions. At an ERG summit hosted in 2019 at its corporate headquarters, Stanley Black & Decker's Black ERG, called African Ancestry, highlighted how they helped to support the company's efforts to provide security solutions to historically Black colleges and universities (HBCUs). The executive sponsor for the African Ancestry

ERG highlighted how he connected ERG members to the sales and marketing team within Stanley Black & Decker assigned to the HBCU accounts. The insights and support provided by the African Ancestry ERG were instrumental in helping the company grow its business with historically Black colleges and universities and thus helped the company meet organizational goals. This was made possible through the brokering role played by their executive sponsor.

Existing Clients

A growing trend within organizations is to leverage their ERGs to strengthen relationships with existing clients, many of which also have ERGs. This typically involves encouraging collaboration and benchmarking between a company's ERGs with the ERGs of top clients. When done effectively, such ERG efforts help to bolster the company's image as a comprehensive solution provider and reinforce key client relationships.

The company regarded as initiating the use of ERGs to strengthen client relationships is Sodexo, the French-owned foodservice and facilities management company whose USA headquarters are in Gaithersburg, Maryland. Sodexo has a longstanding reputation as having best-in-class diversity initiatives and has received many awards for diversity leadership. It is no surprise, then, that the ERGs of Sodexo are also often considered some of the best in the world. One reason is that Sodexo often provides training to their ERG leaders and frequently gathers their ERG leaders for summits and professional development.

Because of its business model, many of Sodexo's employees work on the sites of their top clients because Sodexo provides their foodservice and facilities management services. Many of Sodexo's ERG members are the very employees located on client sites. Their close relationship with clients often resulted in collaborations with the ERGs of their client organizations. These collaborations were encouraged by Sodexo leadership because they further strengthened the client relationship. Because the ERGs of Sodexo tended to be stronger and more strategic than the ERGs of their client organizations, Sodexo ERGs were soon sharing their knowledge and ERG expertise. This helped to build trust and confidence with client organizations who were appreciative of the knowledge sharing by Sodexo ERGs. Demonstrating their diversity leadership, eventually Sodexo saw the value in inviting the ERG members of key clients to their Sodexo ERG summits and professional development sessions. In doing so, the Sodexo ERGs were aligned with the organization's goal of exceeding client expectations. This is because most clients do not anticipate that Sodexo would help strengthen their diversity and inclusion initiatives, which is in addition to their food service and facility management capabilities. The ERGs at Sodexo are highly respected due to their ability to strengthen client relationships.

Incremental Revenue

For-profit companies have sales and revenue goals to meet. This is of no surprise to ERGs. However, some ERGs have strategically and successfully positioned themselves to help drive revenue for the company. This scenario typically exists in organizations that provide services and products directly to consumers. When this occurs, the Commerce name for this 4C pillar really applies.

One such example of a Commerce-related ERG initiative is Uber, the ride-hauling and food delivery company. One of Uber's ERGs is the Immigrants ERG, whose mission is to help build a more-inclusive Uber by providing a welcoming forum for new immigrants and to promote cross-cultural learnings. Uber Eats is one of Uber's business services, which provides an online food-ordering and delivery platform. Uber Eats allows customers to read menus, browse reviews, order, and pay for food from participating restaurants using a web browser application.

As the immigrant population has grown in various parts of the United States, restaurants catering to this growing immigrant segment have also grown. The Immigrants ERG at Uber saw an opportunity to identify restaurants that service immigrant communities but were not participating establishments on the Uber Eats platform. Thus, the Immigrants ERG focused on raising Uber Eats' name recognition within immigrant communities and encouraged them to recommend the food-ordering application to their favorite immigrant restaurants. Ultimately, the Immigrants ERG at Uber was able to help increase the number of restaurants patronized by immigrant populations on the food delivery platform. In doing so, not only did the ERG help to improve food sales of these establishments and increase the number of restaurant options in immigrant communities, but they also helped to drive incremental revenue growth for the organization.

Another example of an employee resource group aligning with revenue generation goals is a retailing organization based in Chicago. Chicago happens to hold one of the biggest gay pride parades in the country. In 2019, which happened to be the fiftieth anniversary of the Chicago gay pride parade, over 1 million spectators watched the parade. The parade consists of approximately 250 entries, which include elaborately decorated floats, politicians in cars, celebrities, performers and entertainers, and various groups of marchers. Often the parade participants give out candy, beads, trinkets, knickknacks, and assorted tchotchkes along the route to the parade spectators. In 2019, the LGBTQ employee resource group at this retailing organization was a parade entrant, and they created a float with the company's logo and the name of their Pride ERG. Members of the retailing company's leadership team, D&I department, and Pride ERG members stood on the float or walked alongside.

However, instead of giving out beads or candy, Pride ERG members handed out coupons with a discount code. Recipients of the coupons could bring it in to one of the company's many retailing locations and redeem the coupon for a small discount on their next purchase. The company handed out over 20,000 coupons during the parade, each costing the company only 0.15 cents to print, for a total cost of $3,000. However, because of the discount code, the company was able to track how many coupons were redeemed and how much revenue was generated by the coupons. In total, the coupons that were distributed during the gay pride parade and redeemed by parade spectators resulted in an incremental revenue lift of close to $300,000. So not only did the gay pride participation by the LGBTQ employee resource group help increase name recognition and reputation within the gay community, the ERG was able to declare that it raised $300,000 in revenue to help the company meet their sales goal and thus align themselves with an organizational objective.

Another way that ERGs can demonstrate organizational alignment is to help tests new company products and/or solution offerings. In doing so, ERGs help an organization catch product defects early, helping to avoid issues that may lead to customer dissatisfaction or product malfunction. Not only does this help to protect users, but it also serves to help protect a company's reputation and integrity. Because ERGs represent mostly women and historically underrepresented groups, they often provide a wonderful internal focus group for an organization whose customers will likely also be women and racial/ethnic minorities. When ERGs test such products, they help to ensure they are viable from a multicultural perspective.

For example, the ERGs at several pharmaceutical companies such as Bristol Myers Squibb, Merck, Baxter, and Johnson & Johnson, to name a few, are actively involved in testing new medicines, vaccines, medical devices, or other medical therapies. Before these products can be made available to the public, they must be tested in humans in studies called clinical trials. Data from clinical trials on a treatment's safety and efficacy is required as a condition of approval by regulatory authorities such as the US Food and Drug Administration. These clinical data provide insights for prescribers about how people are likely to respond to medicines and, therefore, how the medicines may best be used. But differences between people can often lead to different responses to the same medication. Age, genetics, gender, weight, ethnic origin, or race may play a role in how treatment may work or how safe it may be. For this reason, the diversity in clinical trial populations can be critical to public health and well-being through increased representation of populations who experience a certain condition.

People who are underrepresented in health care generally are likely to be underrepresented in clinical research. The barriers may be economic, linguistic, cultural, or even religious. For these reasons, ERGs become an excellent resource in helping their organizations diversify their clinical trial populations. The ERGs at these pharmaceutical companies actively look for ways to increase diversity in clinical trials through a multicultural lens and thus demonstrate organizational alignment.

Business Effectiveness

Aligning with key organizational priorities or goals is not the only way that ERGs can leverage the Commerce pillar. To be successful, organizations also need to be efficient and effective in their day-to-day operations. That means that organizations must strive for the best possible economic results from the resources currently employed or available.

While helping to achieve a big organizational goal may bring more attention to ERGs, their ability to help make an organization more effective daily is equally impactful, albeit less likely to be newsworthy. For example, daily organizations are looking for ways to reduce operational costs. Even little cost savings daily can amount to significant cost reductions in the long run. Here I've seen ERGs direct attention and effort toward opportunities for economically significant results.

Take the daily electricity costs of running an office. If an organization can find a variety of ways to reduce their daily electricity costs, it could amount to huge savings. The ERGs of a small transportation company based in Boston established a goal to help the company reduce its electricity costs. They launched a campaign that was supported by all six of their ERGs to help their company reduce energy costs by 40 percent in one year. They shared information with fellow employees on the benefits of using natural sunlight in offices, as opposed to lights whenever possible. They reminded employees to turn off lights when not in use. They encouraged employees to make it a daily practice that if they noticed an office or meeting room with lights on that were not in use to simply go into the room and shut off the lights. This soon led to the encouragement of turning off computers and office equipment such as printers and copiers when not in use. They also advised office managers to replace old bulbs with more energy-efficient light bulbs. Ultimately, the ERG efforts did help the small company reduce their electricity cost. The following year, they extended this initiative and also helped the company cut down on its use of office paper with similar cost reductions. While these ERG initiatives may not sound glamorous, they do convey that ERGs can help improve the cost effectiveness of an organization and that is not something to take lightly (pun intended).

Today, some companies even have environmental and sustainability ERGs. These sustainability-centered ERGs provide employees with a chance to make an individual, local difference while allowing diverse employees to connect over a shared passion and mission. Some of these ERGs include the Planet ERG at Dell, the Go Green ERG at Macy's, the Environmental Sustainability Employee Network at State Street Corporation, and the Walgreens Environmental Sustainability Network at Walgreens, to name but a few.

Another Commerce pillar initiative that impacts business effectiveness are those that seek to improve the customer experience.

A positive customer experience helps to promote loyalty, helps in customer retention, and encourages brand advocacy. Because of these benefits, organizations are daily trying to avoid a negative customer experience in several ways including poor customer service, difficult purchasing processes, poor quality products, lack of product information, or the feeling of unappreciation as a customer.

Every year, several million people go through the various facilities operated by the Port Authority of New York and New Jersey. These facilities include five airports (such as LaGuardia and John F. Kennedy airports), train stations such as Grand Central, several bus terminals, various bridges and tunnels, the ports of New York and New Jersey, and the World Trade Center. Each person that utilizes and visits each one of the facilities is in essence a customer of the Port Authority of New York and New Jersey (PANYNJ). A total of nine employee business resource groups (EBRGs) exist at the Port Authority. Since 2019, I have worked with the PANYNJ to help their EBRGs achieve excellence. One of their employee business resource groups is called the Port Authority Abilities Network. A Commerce pillar initiative of the Port Authority Abilities Network that promotes business effectiveness is to help enhance the customer experience of individuals with physical disabilities who use the various Port Authority facilities. Periodically, EBRG members of the Port Authority Abilities Network will randomly visit some of the PANYNJ facilities and check for any potential challenges and obstacles that might create a poor or dangerous experience for someone with a physical disability. They identify areas that might not be easily accessible for someone in a wheelchair, they check to see that elevators and escalators are working properly, they seek to isolate areas that might benefit from the installation of a vertical platform lift, they check train platforms to ensure they have smooth edges they determine if facilities are animal friendly for those who might have service animals, and so on. By helping to promote increased accessibility, the Port Authority Abilities Network is enhancing the customer experience, demonstrating yet another example of an ERG supporting Commerce initiatives.

Business effectiveness can also be enhanced by ERGs through quality improvement initiatives. For years, companies have embraced various quality improvement methodologies including Six Sigma, Lean manufacturing, and total quality management (TQM). But not every quality improvement effort needs to be on such a grand scale. Any effort by an employee resource group to improve the quality of a product or service aligns with the Commerce pillar. The Hispanic ERG at an industrial manufacturing organization based in St. Paul recently shared how one of their Latino members came across a document that described one of the company's products in Spanish. The Latino ERG member, being a native Spanish speaker, noticed that the translation was of poor quality and inaccurate. The Hispanic ERG shared this insight with senior management. Soon, someone from the corporate communications department reached out to seek more insights on poor translation. During the discussion, the corporate communications employee shared that the company used various vendors to translate product descriptions into multiple languages. They also shared that throughout the organizations, five different vendors were used to help with Spanish translations. Corporate communications realized that they could work with the Hispanic ERG to help them improve the quality of their Spanish language translations.

In partnership with the Hispanic ERG, corporate communications put together a document that they sent to all five of their Spanish language translation vendors. When each vendor provided the document translated into Spanish, the Hispanic ERG members reviewed the documents. Several of the ERG members were fluent in speaking, reading, and writing in Spanish. After their inspection, the ERG members determined that of the five vendors, only two accurately captured the correct tone, vocabulary, and localized flavor in their translation. With this insight, the corporate communications negotiated volume pricing rates with the two chosen Spanish translation companies and stopped using the other three vendors. This provides an example of an ERG supporting quality control efforts that enhance business effectiveness and impact the Culture pillar.

Similarly, any effort by an ERG to try to diversity an organization's vendor and supplier partners also supports business effectiveness. Organizations place trust on reliable vendors and suppliers to help ensure their operations run smoothly. This provides an opportunity for ERGs to help the company identify and select a more diverse group of suppliers. ERGs can help the company identify suppliers that are certified as women or minority owned businesses. Employee resource groups can connect their company to chambers of commerce affiliated with diverse communities such as the US Hispanic Chamber of Commerce or the National Gay & Lesbian Chamber of Commerce. ERGs can also work with the diverse vendors themselves providing key introductions to leaders in the procurement department, helping the diverse vendor successfully navigate the supplier selection process or simply making diverse vendors aware of upcoming projects that they might be able to bid on. The connection between ERGs and the supplier diversity function has been blossoming over the last decade and it is a trend that must continue as ERGs pursue excellence.

Of the 4C Pillars, ERGs seem to need the most help with the Commerce pillar. Even though several ways to support an organization are outlined in this chapter, ERGs still struggle with this pillar. One reason is that ERG members often feel that supporting business initiatives is beyond the scope of their ERG. Members feel that their day job is the best way for them to support the business and that doing so via ERG initiatives is redundant and likely not the reason they decided to join. But ERG leaders must not waiver. Performing with distinction with Commerce initiatives not only gives the ERGs the credibility and respect that they deserve, but it is also often the final piece in having a holistic value proposition. That is why I consistently advocate for

ERGs to increase the intentionality behind their Commerce-related initiatives. Commerce cannot be the ugly stepchild of the 4C pillars. I often encourage them to establish Commerce pillars as part of their organizational structure.

In my experience, the lack of business alignment or an impact on helping the organization achieve their goals is a reason that more senior-level employees do not join an ERG. To them, why join an ERG that does not help the company succeed? Granted, their view of the impact that an ERG can have is incomplete, but that is not to say their concern is not valid. Closer alignment with organizational goals will help an ERG attract more senior-level leaders. These leaders then cannot only help the ERG with their Commerce pillars but with all four pillars within the 4C Model. Employee resource groups that fail to address the Commerce pillar with distinction do so at their own peril and lessen their probability of achieving ERG excellence.

But before I lay the blame completely on the ERGs for lackluster performance in the Commerce pillar, organizations themselves are equally to blame. I've seen numerous examples of ERGs having a tremendous desire to support the organization. They want to serve as internal focus group members. They desire to be asked to provide input into multicultural marketing campaigns. They wish for increased visibility with the supplier diversity department. They want to help sales initiatives that target diverse client segments. It's as if these ERGs are jumping out and shouting, "Leverage us, we are here to help!" So, the problem is not always for lack of desire or intention by ERGs to support organizational goals. The problem is often lack of understanding by the organization itself of how to leverage ERGs to support their key organizational goals or business effectiveness initiatives. Again, it's as if the organization is telling ERGs, "No thanks. We're fine. We've got it covered. We don't need your help."

When this occurs, ERGs in essence become an underutilized business asset for an organization. Companies must become better able to utilize the most underutilized asset of all, brainpower. The Commerce pillar thus becomes a mechanism to unlock the hidden value that resides in ERGs that is often squandered. Let's use an example to illustrate our point. Consider Uber and Airbnb. Both organizations provide platforms that turn highly underutilized assets into monetization opportunities for sellers. Companies estimate that cars are utilized to the tune of only 4 percent by their owners. For car owners, Uber helps car owners turn their underutilized assets into income-generating opportunities. A person's home is often considered a nonmonetized asset. But Airbnb helped homeowners find a market for their underutilized assets. I believe that as ERGs strive toward excellence, their underutilized status will begin to diminish as organizations seek new ways to generate value. Thus, the organization is also supporting the transformation of ERGs to have a more holistic value proposition.

9 ERG Analytics

Data-Driven Insights

With the prominence of employee resource groups within organizations, it amazes me that analytics and data-driven insights are hardly ever used. To me, this is the missing piece towards achieving ERG excellence. Organizations are simply ill-prepared, or lack the conviction, to utilized analytics to make more data-driven decisions as it relates to their employee resource groups. Given that I hold a doctorate and understand the value of data analysis, it could be that I'm a bit biased on this subject. But it is my belief that the next frontier for ERGs will be the greater utilization of data analytics to measure ERG performance, impact, and analysis.

Organizations must increase the use of data to drive ERG strategy and effective decision-making. Our ERGs must be able to capture data from which they can glean actionable insights. Data analytics encompasses many diverse types of data analysis. Any information can be subjected to data analytics techniques to gain insights that can be used to improve ERGs. Data analytics can help an ERG notice trends and metrics that would otherwise be lost in the mass of information that is flowing every day.

Based on my vast experience of working with hundreds of organizations and their ERGs, I see four distinct types of data analytics that organizations need for their ERGs. First, they need descriptive analytics that describe what has happened to ERGs over a given period of time. This could answer questions as to why ERG membership has gone up. Or why ERG member engagement is down. Second, they need diagnostic analytics that focus more on why something happened within an ERG. This tends to involve more diverse data inputs and a bit of hypothesizing. Did the new Leadership Academy increase ERG leader performance? Did the latest ERG focus group help to improve the customer experience? Third, companies need predictive analytics that seek to convey what is likely going to happen in the immediate future. What happened to ERG performance the last time they launched new field chapters? How much new revenue can we expect if we ERG members give our discount coupons at next year's gay pride parade? Finally, organizations will benefit from prescriptive analytics that suggest a course of action. If we desire an increase in overall employee engagement of 5 percent on the next companywide engagement survey, we should increase the number of intersectionality events run by ERGs by 25 percent.

These sorts of data analytics do not exist within most organizations. At least not yet. It was this lack of analytics as they apply to ERGs that led me to create the 4C ERG Assessment™ several years ago. It allows companies the ability to use data analytics to measure ERG performance and impact in each of the 4C areas. The assessment provides at least some insight into each type of data analytics just described, including descriptive, diagnostic, predictive, and prescriptive data. Yet, the results of the assessment are not presented in an overly academic, scholarly, or quantitative manner. Rather, data is shared in a practical manner that is easy to understand, and more importantly, provides insights that an organization can apply immediately to improve ERG performance.

To me, this new assessment model has been needed for a long time in order to capture the growing sophistication of today's next-generation ERGs. What was needed was an assessment tool that allows firms to determine the current state of their ERGs yet doesn't create the false belief that an ERG will improve and mature over time. This assessment philosophy allows for a more accurate reflection of ERG performance, one more dependent on the environment in which the ERG operates, and on who is leading the ERG, as opposed to simply how long the ERG has been in existence, which is often the focus of more maturity-based models.

An assessment methodology that measures ERG performance across different elements independently of each other was needed. Without the ability to assess different elements independently, firms run the greater risk of inflating ERG performance in some areas while underestimating performance results in other areas.

For example, at a large managing consulting firm, the ERGs were off-the-charts effective in creating community, contributing to a greater culture of inclusion, and creating developmental opportunities for their members. But they were invisible – and therefore irrelevant – to the organization's drive for marketplace growth. At a packaged goods company, the converse was true. The ERGs had gotten so effective and valued at contributing to marketplace insights that they had begun to flag in their social engagement – a vital influencer of member participation.

An independent assessment approach the 4C Model follows allows firms to measure ERG effectiveness simultaneously in the areas of business impact (of importance to corporate executives), career enhancement (of paramount importance to ERG members), and civic impact (of importance to the communities an ERG serves). The ability to benchmark data across companies is key. How do ERGs perform against the ERGs at other companies? Within the same industry? How do certain ERGs compare to the same networks at other firms? Without the ability to benchmark, it's all a guessing game—one that leads to the creation of programs and initiatives in a vacuum. Conversely, benchmarking allows ERGs to bust out of ruts by identifying new ways of addressing their members' needs. When ERGs don't benchmark, they confine their possibilities.

A diversity leader at a major consumer packaged-goods company in New Jersey using the 4C Model and conducting the 4C Assessment found that each of his company's ERGs had progressed at a different rate. More specifically, he found that within each ERG, some strategy elements were operating very effectively, while others were not. By rejecting the assumption that each ERG matured at the same rate and that within each ERG every strategy element was equally effective, the company was able to develop specific plans not only for each ERG, but for each element of strategy.

Michael Escobar, former chief diversity officer at Allstate Insurance Company, was relatively new to his role when he decided he needed more information about the current state of his company's ERGs. Allstate used the 4C ERG Assessment™ to gain a holistic perspective on just how well each ERG was doing. But of greater importance was Escobar's desire to evaluate each ERG from a different stakeholder's perspective. Thus, each was evaluated not only based on the ERG member perspective, but also on the perspective of executive sponsors. In addition, Allstate assessed the ERGs from the point of view of each business unit within the company, something that had never been done before within the organization. Finally, the assessment tool allowed Escobar to see how the ERGs at Allstate compared to ERGs at other corporations. Armed with this insight, Allstate now had useful assessment data that informs its ERG strategy plus key aspects of its overall diversity strategy.

As of 2021, approximately 250 proactive corporations, from a variety of industries, have followed Allstate's approach and completed the 4C Assessment including companies such as Uber, Asurion, Liberty Mutual, LinkedIn, Stanley Black & Decker, Levi Strauss, SurveyMonkey, the Federal Reserve Bank, Under Armour,

FiatChrysler, Verizon, SC Johnson, Gallo Winery, NBCUniversal, and State Street Corporation to name just a few. On average, each company assesses about eight ERGs and about 350 employees typically participate in each company survey. All these survey responses feed into the 4C Assessment normative database that now has over 75,000 individual data-points all associated with ERG performance. All this data is mined for analytic purposes using a proprietary algorithm and provides insights on both the collective current state of ERGs in corporate America as well as insights on individual ERGs as a company.

The 4C ERG Assessment process is quite simple. The first step is to determine cuts of the data that an organization may desire. The most often selected cuts of the data by organizations include by ERG, by location, by ERG role, by job level, and by business unit. When the assessment results are shared with an organization, they are done so by each selected data cut. The second step is simply collecting the data from ERG members. This is simply done via a weblink that can be distributed to ERG members so they can complete the assessment by answering an online questionnaire. I mostly tend to use SurveyMonkey to collect ERG responses to the assessment, but some organizations insist on using their own internal platforms to collect assessment responses. Every company that completes the 4C ERG Assessment answers the same set of questions, which allows for benchmarking analysis.

Once the data is collected, it is organized and fed into my proprietary software algorithm, which provides the statistical analysis. This process is what compares the results for any individual company's ERG Assessment results against the ERG Assessment results of all the other organizations in the normative database. The algorithm then determines where the organization's ERG Assessment results fell in comparison to all the other assessment scores. It is like being graded on a bell-shaped curve, like when you were back in school. Figure 9.1 shows the normal distribution resulting from the algorithm.

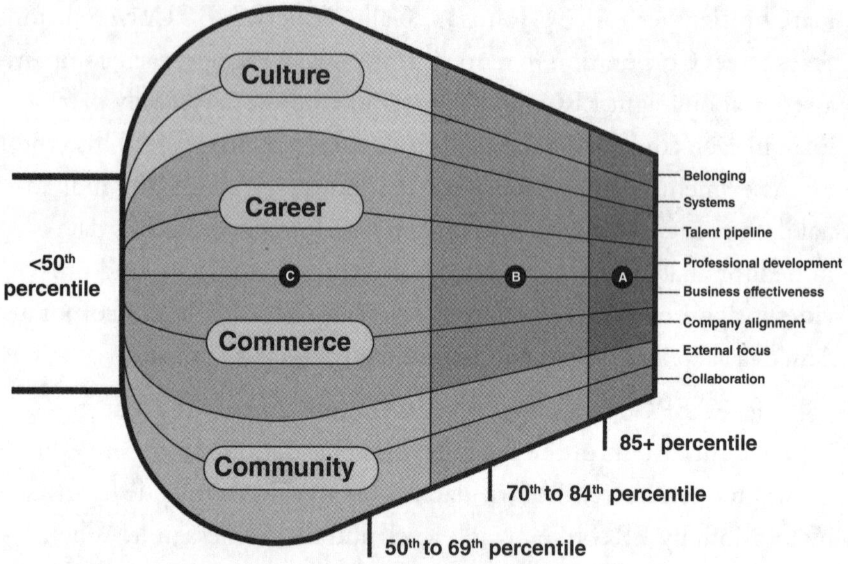

Figure 9.1 4C ERG Assessment: Normal Distribution

Finally, the ERG results are placed in a tier system, depending on where scores fell in comparison to all the other scores on the database. The ERG Assessment scores are then plotted on a circumplex for easy interpretation of the results. Figure 9.2 shows a comparison between two ERGs within the same organization and how they scored on each of the 4C areas.

The insights provided to an organization are tremendous and provide valuable quantitative and qualitative information that can be utilized to make more data-driven decisions for ERGs. The 4C ERG Assessment results validate, using quantitative data, what organizations maybe already knew about their ERGs but in only an anecdotal capacity. Or the 4C Assessment results provide amazingly clear new insights that were previously unknown to the organization. The 4C ERG Assessment results are then summarized, shared, and put into a report that includes recommended actions the company should take based on the results.

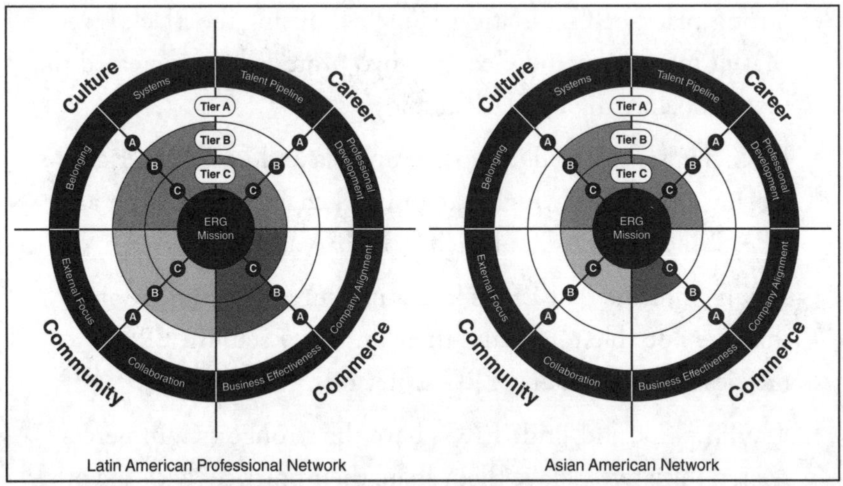

Figure 9.2 4C ERG Assessment™: ERG Comparison

Below is a small sample of 10 ERG insights gleaned from results taken from organizations that completed the 4C ERG Assessment in 2020. They provide an illustration of the data-driven insights that organizations can obtain from their assessment results.

- Early indications of burnout by current ERG leaders, which encourages an increased sense of urgency in ERG leader succession planning to ensure leadership continuity.
- ERG members in field locations are feeling undersupported compared to ERG members at corporate headquarters. Increase ERG field engagement initiatives.
- Women's ERG Career initiatives are providing a strong pipeline of upwardly mobile talent within the ERG. Replicate these Career-related pillars across the other ERGs.
- ERG members who work in Finance are scoring considerably lower than ERG members in other departments. This is likely due to lack of support by leaders in the finance function.
- Overall, the ERGs have strong Collaboration scores. Leverage this to increase the amount of intersectionality events held by the ERG.

- Strong Black ERG initiatives launched during the Black Lives Matter movement and George Floyd protests have increased the sense of belonging by Black employees.
- ERG chapters located in North America and Latin America are scoring considerably higher than ERG chapters in EMEA and APAC. Increase ERG outreach in EMEA and APAC.
- Results indicate that ERGs lack a measurement strategy and thus are not able to capture their impact. Establish ERG metrics-that-matter and ERG scorecards.
- The Hispanic and Pride ERGs have the strongest Commerce-related initiatives. Have them share their practices with the other ERGs to elevate their commerce impact.
- Overall sense of dissatisfaction in professional development sessions provided by all the employee resource groups. Partner with the learning and development department to conduct a learning needs analysis within the ERG membership.

For the first time ever, companies now have data-driven analytics based on an ERG normative database, from which they can make more strategic decisions. Also, the assessment allows companies to establish a baseline of ERG performance from which they can then measure progress if they complete the assessment again. Most organizations that complete the 4C ERG Assessment have their employee retake the assessment again every two to three years to measure their progress. The 4C ERG Assessment is the only data analytics and assessment instrument in the market today.

Normative Database Mining

Because the 4C ERG Assessment has allowed me to capture tons of data related to employee resource groups, I am able to mine the data to extract and discover ERG patterns in this large data set. The key is to obtain information from the ERG data and transform that information into actionable insights that organizations and ERGs can use. This allows organizations to learn more about their ERGs and thus develop more effective strategies to enhance their performance in a more optimal and data-driven manner.

In my work so far with this large ERG normative data set, I've been able to discover these seven statistically driven insights regarding ERGs as a whole and will describe each below.

ERG Leadership Roles Need to Be Highly Desired

If it is difficult to get employees to serve as the chair or president of your ERGs, the data within the normative database indicates that your ERGs will have a difficult time making a tremendous impact. Our data shows a very high correlation between top-tier ERGs and those who score high on the 4C Assessment question "Our ERG leadership roles are highly desired and coveted." This means companies need to design ERG leader roles that are meaningful and provide many benefits to the leader. If you need to convince or beg people to take an ERG leader role, our analytics indicate your ERGs will underperform.

In too many instances, I've seen a leadership role for an ERG open only to have very few ERG members express strong interest in the role. It is possible that these ERG members may secretly harbor a desire for the role but do not wish to appear too ambitious in proclaiming their aspiration. More likely is that when ERG members see the amount of work and responsibility that goes with running an ERG, they become concerned they may not have the bandwidth or time to allocate sufficient time and energy to excel in the role. It is also possible that they have seen previous ERG leaders struggle to gain traction for their ideas on where to steer their ERGs from the membership or are concerned that they may not be supported adequately by the diversity and inclusion function. If they are ultimately convinced, cajoled, or "voluntold" to accept the role of ERG leader, they often underperform.

There are several things that organizations can do to increase the desirability of ERG leadership roles. First, make it a top expectation of current ERG leaders to quickly identify and help groom their replacement. This is the "leader developing leaders" approach. When people feel they are being groomed and prepared for the ERG leadership role, they are more likely to perform with distinction in that role. Next, clearly outline the benefits of serving as an ERG leader. This will help to negate the time commitment and workload concerns many ERG members have when considering applying for the ERG leader role. By outlining the many benefits that result from an ERG leadership role, it is likely potential candidates won't pull themselves out of consideration simply because of the amount of work involved with such a role. Third, establish an ERG Leadership Academy where ERG leaders are given the development they need in order to perform well in their ERG leadership role. Not only does this help ensure ERG leader success, but it conveys to others that they will be supported once in those roles.

The insight for diversity and inclusion is that they need to do more to make the ERG leadership roles desirable. Additional compensation or perks might help, but I see greater value in highlighting the increased visibility and exposure that an ERG leadership role provides to the occupant who has really helped to heighten the desirability of these roles.

Appoint Your ERG Leaders to Top Grade the Role

Our analysis shows that ERGs tend to only be as strong as their ERG leaders. This is why we are seeing more and more corporations move towards appointing the ERG leaders as opposed to allowing ERGs to elect their own leaders. An appointment process improves the probability that a strong performer will hold the ERG leader role. Top-tier ERGs tend to score very high on the survey question "Our ERG has strong performers in the top ERG leadership role." Additionally, the data indicates that when companies appoint their ERG leaders, the ERG leader roles become more desirable and coveted.

The one approach that appears to be the most effective is when organizations align the ERG leadership role with their talent management initiatives. In doing so, the ERG leadership roles are assessed for their developmental components. In doing so, they can leverage the ERG leader role to help groom and prepare their future leaders. The result is that the ERG leader roles tend to be filled by individuals considered to be high performers and high potentials. These leaders tend to be a magnate for other strong leaders. By being able to attract more leaders into the ERG, our data indicates the overall performance of the ERGs improves. Also, resistance from middle management tends to decline when ERGs have top performers with a high level of credibility in the leadership role. This is likely to occur because middle managers tend to have a sense of who within the organization are seen as future stars. When they see that these individuals are now running the ERGs, their sentiment toward ERGs tends to improve, and so does their general support for ERGs.

ERGs Are an Underutilized Asset

As was discussed in Chapter 8, organizations often blame the ERGs for not making a big enough impact on the obtainment of business goals. Some organizations even change the names of the ERGs from employee resource groups to business resource groups (BRGs) in the hopes that this alone will help make sure that the ERGs are not seen as only social groups. However, the 4C normative database indicates that ERGs want to support business goals and they are often proactive in reaching out to business units to find ways to help. The real reason that ERGs don't make a business impact is that the business units don't know how to best utilize the groups. The result is that ERGs sit idly by and are underutilized by the company to provide business value.

Interestingly enough, a trend and correlation within the normative database indicates that the ERG that seem to be pulled into business meetings and are asked to support business goals the most often appear to be the Hispanic ERGs. This is likely due to the fast growth of the Hispanic consumer market and companies realizing their Hispanic ERG members can provide valuable insights to penetrate that market.

For diversity and inclusion professionals, the implication of this insight is that they should encourage executive sponsors to focus more on their role as a strategist and an evangelist. By serving as a strategist, the executive sponsor is pushing ERGs to have more direct alignment with organizational goals. This tends to increase their Commerce initiatives via a push approach. Also, executive sponsors serve as an evangelist when they visibly advocate for ERGs. This advocacy for ERGs can encourage hesitant business and functional leaders to explore ways that they can partner ERGs to meet their goals. This is more of a pull approach in utilizing ERGs toward having a greater business impact and thus unlocking some of their hidden value to an organization.

Professional Development Across the Career Continuum Is Lacking

ERGs tend to score well in the area of professional development by employees who are individual contributors, specialists, and entry-level managers. However, when employees who take the assessment indicate they are at the senior manager, director level, or above, their survey scores on professional development questions are extremely low. This indicates that the professional development needs for more senior-level employees are not adequately addressed by ERGs. When this happens, ERGs no longer become relevant to senior-level employees and they tend to leave the group or not join in the first place. This can have a devasting effect on an ERG in two ways. First, they are not able to attract senior leaders to their ERG, thus limiting the overall intellectual firepower within ERGs. Second, the ERGs end up with a reputation within the organization that indicates that ERG membership is good but only for those at lower levels within the organization and that they are not relevant to more senior leaders. Once this reputation is set, it is hard for ERGs to change it.

What this means is that ERGs need to periodically review their professional development offerings to see if they address topics that are helpful to more senior-level employees and not just focus on meeting professional development needs of more junior employees. Again, insights gleaned from mining the ERG normative database indicate that the Women's ERGs tend to score highest in the Career pillar with strong scores in both the area of professional development and talent pipeline. It would serve an organization well to have other ERGs benchmark with the Women's ERGs to try to replicate their approach within the Career pillar.

ERGs Are Not Benchmarking Adequately

There are several questions on the assessment that focus on the level of benchmarking ERGs do with employee resource groups at other companies. The response is surprisingly low, with many ERGs indicating they do very little to almost no benchmarking with external ERGs. Low scores on the benchmarking scores tend to be highly correlated with overall low scores on the 4C Assessment. Benchmarking helps ERGs learn best practices, find ways to collaborate, and gain insights into potential solutions to common ERG challenges. Companies should encourage their ERGs to reach out and try to connect with ERG leaders at other corporations and to try to establish regular meetings for benchmarking purposes.

While there are many organizations that have taken the 4C ERG Assessment, there are many more organizations that have not taken the assessment. This means most of these organizations have no real access to external benchmarks regarding ERG performance. Some rely on "Top ERG" list but those mostly subjective with substantive quantitative analysis conducted. Often winners of these Top ERG awards tend to be those companies that are strong sponsors of the organization putting together the list of top ERGs, resulting in a perceived pay-to-play scenario. Since the 4C ERG Assessment is the only diagnostic tool on the market for ERGs with a large data set, it is really the only truly comprehensive ERG benchmarking mechanism in existence providing benchmark data in each of the 4C areas.

Whether an organization utilizes the 4C ERG Assessment or not, they should encourage their ERGs to formally benchmark with other ERGs. For example, approximately 40 companies in the greater Chicagoland area have their Latino ERG leaders meet on a quarterly basis. The group, called the Consortium of Latino Employee Organizations (CLEO), rotates who will host the quarterly meeting, and each time they meet they focus on particular topic, such as raising member engagement or establishing metrics-that-matter. The CLEO group in Chicago has met every quarter for the past 10 years, and now a CLEO group in the San Francisco/Silicon Valley area has launched to promote similar benchmarking.

Not All Business Units Value ERGs

As mentioned earlier, when completing a 4C Assessment, companies get to select various cuts of the data for their results. Common data cuts include by ERG, location, job level, and by ERG role. A data cut that has been adopted by an increasing number of companies is to have employees participating in the 4C ERG Assessment indicate their business unit. The result has provided very valuable insights to companies. By reviewing the 4C results by business unit, companies can better determine which parts of the organization are more supportive of their ERG efforts than others. Recently, one client found that the employees who were in one particular business unit scored very low on the assessment. Upon further follow-up, the company was able to determine that the majority of managers in this particular business unit felt that ERGs were not helpful, a waste of time, and they did not support their employees' involvement in ERGs. With this insight, diversity and HR leaders were able to hold a series of meetings with the leaders in this business unit to clarify the importance of ERGs. Without this insight from the 4C Assessment, diversity leaders would not have known about the lack of support for ERG in this part of the organization. An analysis of the normative database indicates that in general, employees in the sales function and in call centers tend to receive the least amount of support from their managers regarding ERG involvement. Employees in information technology and marketing tend to receive the most ERG support.

Career and Commerce Are Key

The 4C Model does not place more importance on any one of the 4C areas (Career, Community, Culture, and Commerce) over the other. However, an analysis of the results in the 4C Assessment database does provide two interesting points for consideration. First, when companies score high on their Career-related questions, it is more likely that they will be able to maintain or improve the scores in the other three areas. It's as if the Career portion of the 4C Model is a driver for the other three areas.

Second, when ERGs score low in the Commerce-related questions, they have difficulty attracting top talent to their ERGs and the ERGs are not given the credibility and respect they deserve. Without strong Commerce scores, ERGs tend to be characterized as mostly social entities by others, thus making it difficult to attract top talent or to make a significant business impact. The implication of this insight is that diversity and inclusion professionals, who often provide oversight for their ERGs, should elevate the priority of Career and Commerce pillars if they perceive their ERGs are struggling.

The 4C Assessment and its normative database contain plenty of data for analysis, resulting in ERG insights. The insights shared here are just some of the many interesting findings that can help companies make smarter business decisions related to their ERGs. ERG data mining is critical in the analytical discovery process and is key to predicting future ERG outcomes, uncovering improvement opportunities, increasing member engagement, and elevating ERG impact to the business and its members. Forward-thinking organizations that have completed the 4C Assessment are leveraging the insights as a competitive differentiator to solve today's toughest ERG challenges.

4C Assessment Case Study: Allstate Corporation

The Allstate Corporation is one of the largest insurance providers in the United States and one of the largest that is publicly held. Based in Northfield, Illinois, the company employs over 83,000 employees and insurance agents. A big part of their success includes a strong company commitment to diversity and inclusion.

In 2012, the Inclusive Diversity Department at Allstate was looking to gain more insights into the current level of performance for their six ERGs. In particular, they sought a better sense of how well each of the ERGs was performing and how to elevate the impact of their ERGs. Plus, they also wanted to establish a baseline of ERG performance so they could better determine if future changes were making a positive impact. Finally, they wanted to gain a better sense of how well their ERGs were doing when compared to ERGs at other companies.

To gain these insights and to establish the performance baseline they desired, Allstate decided to conduct the 4C ERG Assessment in 2012 on all six of their employee resource groups. Approximately 200 employees completed the initial 4C Assessment in 2012.

When their 4C scores were placed on the 4C circumplex, their results indicated that their ERGs had a solid foundation and were well positioned for future growth and elevated impact. However, the 4C Assessment results provided eight key insights that warranted special consideration:

1. There was a wide variance of performance and impact among their six ERGs. (See Figure 9.3.)
2. The ERGs seemed heavily focused on Culture-related initiatives.
3. There were very low levels of collaboration and partnering among the ERGs.
4. Low Commerce scores indicated the ERGs were not making a significant impact on the business.
5. The ERGs appeared to be successful at grooming talent, but they were not necessarily successful at attracting existing senior-level talent into the ERGs.
6. There was a lack of satisfaction across the board with regards to professional development by the ERG members.
7. When the results were analyzed by business units, some units scored very low.
8. There appeared to be low levels of support by middle management of the ERGs.

(continued)

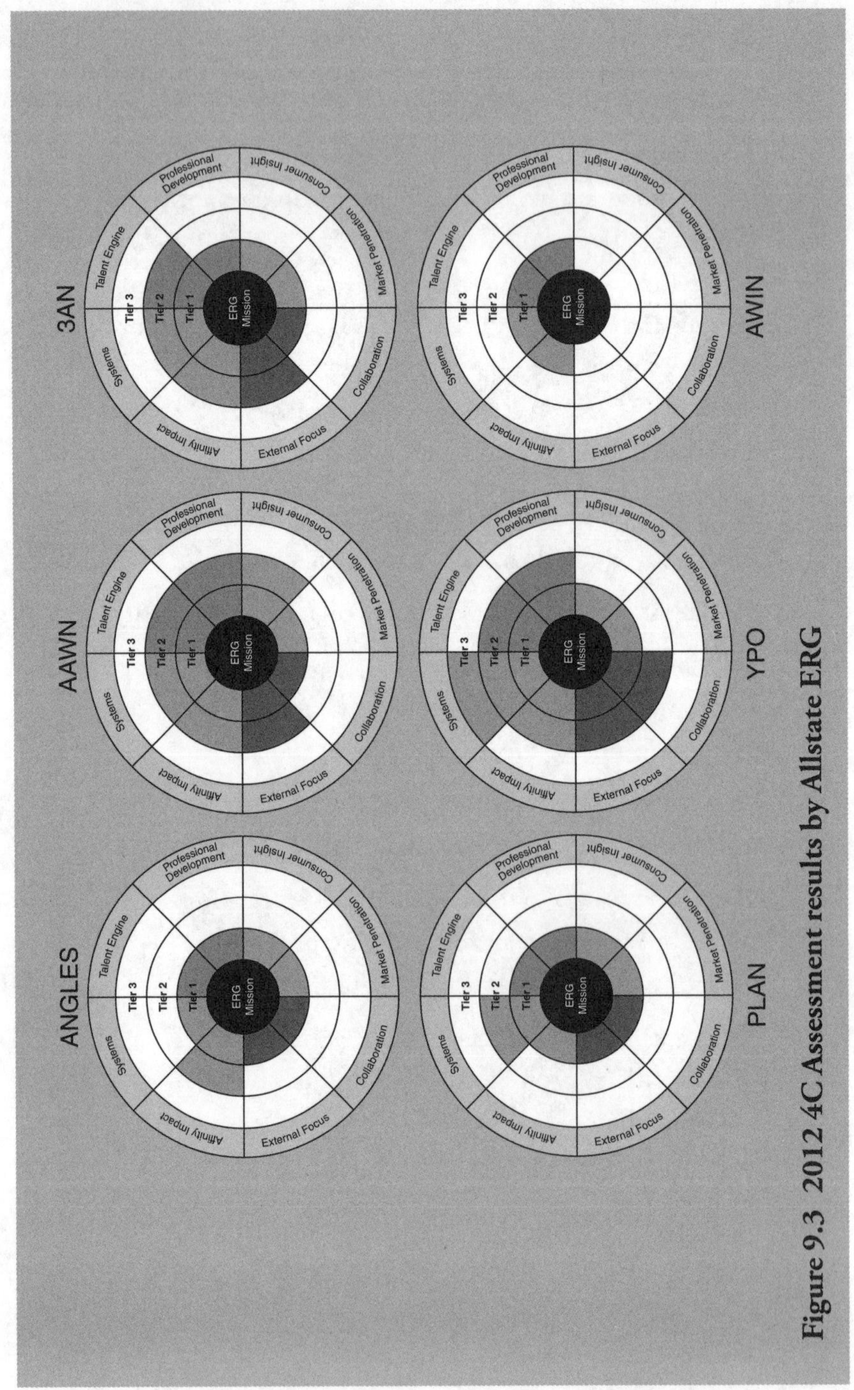

Figure 9.3 2012 4C Assessment results by Allstate ERG

As a result of the insights provided by the 4C Assessment, Allstate implemented several of the recommendations in the 4C Assessment results report. Of most concern was the low level of collaboration among the ERGs. Allstate put systems in place that encouraged the ERGs to work more collaboratively and to partner on major ERG events. They particularly worked more closely with the leaders of the lower-performing ERGs. And finally, they conducted additional analysis into why the 4C scores were so low among employees who worked in certain business units and locations.

After implementing these initial changes, Allstate conducted the 4C Assessment again in 2013. This time, 338 employees completed the 4C Assessment, and the results showed that the ERGs were indeed collaborating more effectively. They also were able to track improvement by some of the lower-performing ERGs. The focus now shifted to raising awareness of the ERGs within the Allstate business units to help them better understand how the ERGs could help them meet their business goals.

An additional 4C Assessment was conducted in 2014. This time, over 500 employees completed the assessment. The results indicated that the number of employees involved in the ERGs had increased. Also, the assessment results indicated that the ERGs were able to sustain their strong scores in the Culture and Community areas with continued improvement in ERG collaboration. However, improvement was proving more difficult in the areas of Commerce and Careers.

(continued)

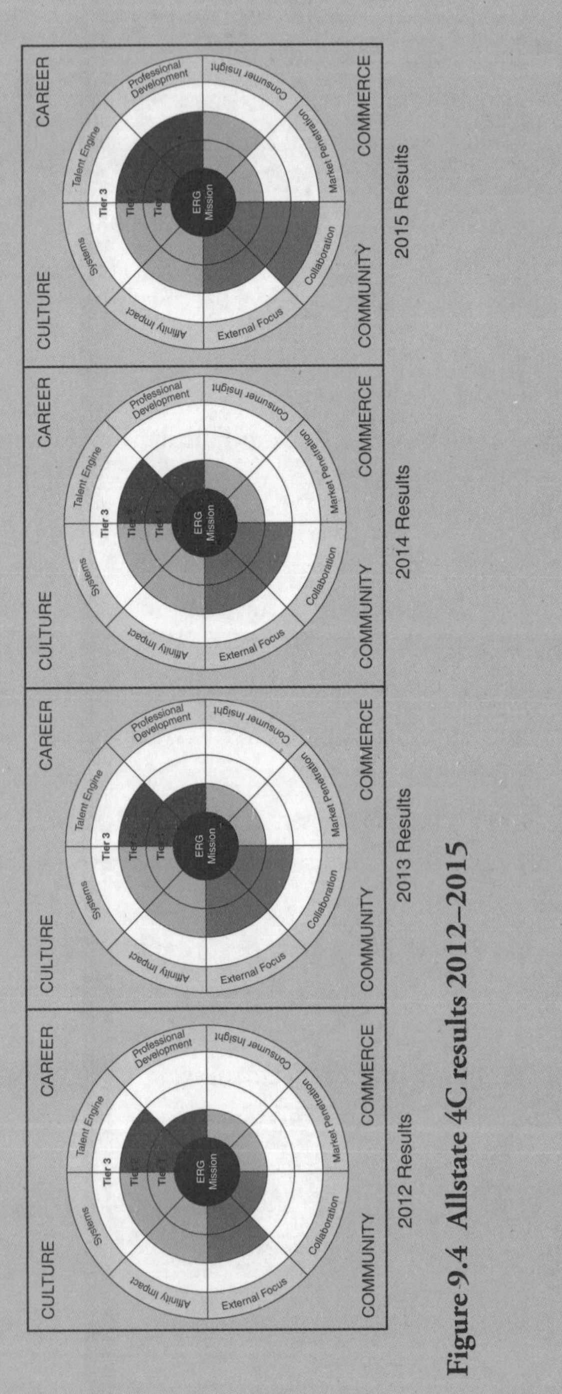

Figure 9.4 Allstate 4C results 2012–2015

Allstate launched the ERG Leadership Academy to provide its ERG leaders with improved skills in the areas of problem solving, decision-making, strategic thinking, and effective meeting management. As the capabilities of their ERG leaders increased, the performance and impact of the ERGs increased as well. A fourth 4C Assessment was conducted in 2015, and the results showed significant improvements in the areas of professional development. Not only were the ERGs at Allstate helping to groom future talent, but the ERGs were now attracting more individuals who were already considered to be senior leaders within the company.

Additionally, the ERGs were now being invited to provide more insights on how to better connect with diverse market segments by business unit leaders. This resulted in improved scores in the Commerce area mostly driven by the increase use of ERGs to provide consumer insights. And finally, the 4C Assessment indicated that Allstate was performing at the "Best-in-Class" level when it came to collaboration among their ERGs. When comparing their 4C results on a year-by-year basis, the results indicated that the ERGs had significantly improved their performance and impact in a short period of time (see Figure 9.4).

Based on the valuable insights provided by the 4C Assessment, Allstate encouraged one of its newly acquired businesses to conduct the 4C Assessment on its ERGs. Esurance, an Allstate-owned company, conducted the 4C Assessment on its ERGs in 2016. By using the 4C Model and Assessment, eSurance was not only able to gain insights into their ERGs, but they were also better able to align their ERG initiatives with those of their new parent company.

(continued)

By implementing the 4C Model and conducting the 4C Assessment, Allstate was able to:

- Establish a baseline for ERG performance, thus allowing them to track future progress.
- Gain data-driven insights that allowed them to make better business decisions related to their ERGs.
- Uncover specific areas of improvement specific to each ERG.
- Better understand how their ERGs not only compare to each other, but how their ERGs compare to ERGs at other corporations.
- Increase ERG alignment across the Allstate enterprise, including wholly owned business entities.
- Enhance the capabilities of their ERG leaders.
- Establish their ERGs as capable of providing important insights to business unit leaders.

The 4C Assessment was critically instrumental in helping Allstate improve the performance and impact of its ERGs. Using data to capture the current state of its ERGs, Allstate was able to map out a strategy that led to sustainable improvements that could be replicated across its various ERGs and scaled to the entire Allstate enterprise. The ERGs at Allstate have recently won awards, cementing their reputation as some of the best ERGs in corporate America.

10 ERG Metrics-That-Matter

Measuring ERG Impact and Excellence

An employee resource group cannot strive toward excellence if it does not have a means of determining if it is making progress. Nor can an ERG determine the impact and value it provides to an organization without some sort of measurement strategy. Yet in my experience, most employee resource groups simply capture metrics related to their activity. They are quick to share how many members they have, the number of events they held, or the size of the audience at their meetings.

While this may be a nice start, it is far from a comprehensive measurement strategy. Of course, ERGs need to capture their activity and share it with their stakeholders. It allows them to highlight what the group has been up to and gives them a quantitative measure of their endeavors for a specific period of time. But the journey toward ERG excellence requires more than just measuring activity. Employee resource groups have to find ways to capture the impact of those activities and the effect their initiatives have on their membership, the organization, and on the broader community. Without the ability to articulate ERG impact, it is more difficult to counter critics who still see the groups as only social entities.

Along with measuring impact, ERG metrics help a group determine their progress. To do this, an ERG must have a metric or measurement that allows it to establish a baseline or starting point. Once the baseline is established, the ERG can then determine if improvement or growth has occurred by taking measurements again and comparing it to the baseline. Without the ability to track movement, an ERG has no way of knowing if it is moving forward or plateauing, or if things have regressed. Tracking progress allows ERGs to know if they are moving in the right direction. Plus, without regular tracking of how an ERG is doing, there is no way of knowing whether ERG initiatives are moving them closer to their desired goals or task completion.

Tracking progress enables ERGs to improve their ability to estimate when they will reach certain goals and helps them gain credibility with their members and their executive sponsor. Tracking the progress of various metrics definitely takes discipline and a certain level of comfort in capturing information and data. But ultimately, having measurement discipline allows an ERG to improve its efficiency and effectiveness. When data and metrics are used to track progress, ERGs are less likely to lose the attention of their stakeholders.

Ultimately, the strongest benefit of having a strong measurement strategy is that it allows ERGs to better tell their story. Humans have always told stories, and they are a vital part of our daily communication. But stories have meaning beyond entertainment value. In fact, storytelling is a strong business skill, and when implemented effectively, it can boost an ERG in a number of ways, such as improving member engagement, attracting allies, and conveying impact. Storytelling with metrics conveys purpose and ERGs with purpose are noticed and win the loyalty of stakeholders. It is not enough for an ERG to simply exist; an ERG needs to stand out, and metrics provide a mechanism for doing just that.

Leveraging metrics and data helps ERGs persuade audiences to buy into their overall mission. When ERG metrics are organized in a logical manner, these metrics support the often-persuasive arguments that ERGs are trying to make about the benefits of a having a diverse workforce. This is particularly useful when trying to share the sophisticated approach taken by ERGs by non-ERG members and middle managers. Storytelling through data provides context so that coworkers understand why your ERG is worth supporting and joining.

Communicating and persuading effectively with data and storytelling is a crucial skill for anyone who wants to lead in a modern organization. Metrics help others visualize what an ERG is trying to achieve and thus conveys a more compelling story. People tend to remember stories and thus metrics help ERGs engage their stakeholders. Stories have the power to charm and influence and even change behavior. ERGs operate in a world increasingly dominated by data. Data are used to make important decisions, to shape business and diversity policies, and to understand the fundamental workings of systems within a workplace.

When ERG mission statements are merely listed on a charter, very few people tend to remember what the mission is, what it means, and how the work of an ERG is reflected in daily workplace behavior. It can be through storytelling and the use of metrics that ERG leaders can connect, align, and inspire others. Stories, when coupled with compelling metrics, are credible and absorbing; they build rapport, inspire action, explain complex diversity challenges, and spread messages through viral retelling. While it may seem counterintuitive, metrics and storytelling go hand in hand and help to build an emotional connection with ERGs.

I have seen metrics tell a variety of stories. Some stories change opinions and overcome objections because they not only provide hard facts, but also make a case for a new perspective and give a call to action. Thus, the effective use of data makes a case for a new perspective. Data can seed doubts about the old worldview; thus, critics become open to new realities. I've heard ERG members tell stories of success by introducing the emotions that employees felt before an ERG existed and how their lives have improved since. How they went from feeling frustrated working at the company to feeling inspired and excited.

Some ERGs shy away from metrics and capturing data because they find measurements complicated, mysterious, and difficult to make others understand. That's where dashboards and scorecards come in. Metric dashboards function to provide real-time results by aggregating and extracting value from all the data an ERG can collect. A well-constructed dashboard simplifies data into more manageable chucks of visual information that allows ERGs to show what they are doing and how well they are doing. When utilized properly, ERGs can use a dashboard to make informed decisions that dramatically impact performance.

In my extensive work with employee resource groups, I've captured the 50 most used ERG metrics within organizations. While some of these metrics simply capture activity, others measure impact. But before we explore some of these more common metrics, let's first discuss some key principles about metrics in general.

Key Measurement Principles

The first principle employee resource groups need to know about metrics is that you can't fix what you don't measure. The belief stems from a belief that if you can't measure something, you cannot manage it. Also, if you cannot measure it, you cannot improve it. These beliefs stem from the renowned management guru Edward Deming. I believe these concepts absolutely must be applied by employee resource groups. To properly manage an ERG, leaders need to know what's happening. Metrics allow ERGs to know what is happening.

For instance, I often hear ERG leaders say, "Member engagement is low," or "Middle management support is lacking." To which my response is usually, "Well, how do you know that?" This is usually followed by a look of puzzlement or reference to some anecdotal piece of evidence from which they draw this conclusion. My advice for employee resource groups is to try to put together a metric or measurement for things you believe are critical to the success of the ERG. The metrics will thus provide the evidence that will inform what is happening within the employee resource group.

The second principle I recommend ERGs follow is that they shouldn't assume linear growth or improvement in all their metrics. Often, things need to plateau or dip before they improve. It is not too uncommon for ERG leaders to get shaken quickly if they don't see immediate improvement in particular metrics. Worse still is when they see a drop in a metric that they expected to increase. Certain things take time to for positive change happens. ERG leaders often assume that every metric once in place will improve in a direct manner.

Consider the experience of an ERG at a health care organization based in California. Their ERG lobbied their organization to allow them to have a social media page for their employee resource group. Once approval was granted, the ERG set up both a Twitter and Instagram social media page for their ERG. At first, the number of followers and "likes" on their social media accounts grew quickly. But after about a month, the pace of growth in followers and likes dropped significantly, resulting in a new flurry of postings by the ERG. However, new followers and likes were slow to come. The leaders of the ERG believed that they might be doing something wrong, or that they needed to post something provocative that would attract increased interest. After their initial panic subsided, the ERGs realized that it simply takes time for a social media page to find the right followers and establish its niche. Eventually, more followers came, and the likes increased but the growth was more gradual but still significant.

The third principle ERGs must remember is that not all metrics mature or improve at the same rate. An ERG can launch initiatives in several areas, but they should not expect that each will yield positive results within the same timeframe. Worse still, improvement in one area will not necessarily result in improvement in another. One ERG that I worked with had two recent metrics they hoped would improve simultaneously. One was new ERG member growth and the other was an increase in the number of members who volunteered for their community day initiative. In a year-over-year analysis, the ERG did notice an increase in membership of 15 percent. However, when comparing the metric regarding the number of volunteers for their community day activity, there was no growth during the same time frame. Instead of mistakenly believing that their community day was less popular, they had to come to the realization that growing the number of volunteers required more direct outreach and that a larger membership base would not necessarily result in a larger number of volunteers.

Yet another principle to remember is that different stakeholders have different needs. What is important to one stakeholder may not be as important to another stakeholder. Therefore, ERGs need different metrics to track those things that are important to their various stakeholders. Consider that for an ERG leader, overall membership growth might be an important metric. It shows that their initiatives are attracting a larger number of employees to become members. However, for their executive sponsor, membership growth may not be important at all. They may have more interest in the growth of "active" members versus members who are not active. Their belief may be that it does not benefit the ERG to have more members if those members are not active. For ERG members themselves, they may be less concerned with having more members overall as they are in growing members in certain locations. They may want membership growth to come from field offices so that they can have more chapters, as opposed to wanting more members at the corporate office. The message here is to have a variety of metrics that appeal to different stakeholders.

The final principle that I recommend ERG leaders understand is that it is critically important to establish a baseline from which you can measure ERG progress using metrics. For ERG purposes, a baseline provides a number or metric that represents the current state of something before initiatives begin that are intended to improve the measurement. This allows an employee resource group to track progress and to capture a snapshot of intended improvement at any given time. Without an established metric baseline, it is difficult to gauge movement in the metric.

Consider an initiative intended to improve the number of new employee referrals given by ERG members. The first step would be to determine how many employee referrals an ERG makes in a given year without any specific initiative to increase the number of referrals. If, for example, an ERG averages 5–10 employee referrals by ERG members each year, it has now established a baseline from which to measure progress. Now an ERG can announce the initiative to grow employee referrals by making members aware of the referral process, streamlining the employee referral process, or even creating an incentive to encourage ERG members to make employee referrals. After launching the ERG referral initiative, they can now track the number of referrals made in the year since the launch of the initiative. If, for example, the number of ERG employee referrals is now 40 in a given year, they are able to show that their efforts have resulted in a significant increase in ERG employee referrals. Without having established the baseline, there is no way of knowing if the 40 ERG referrals made since the launch of the initiative resulted in an actual increase in referrals.

ERG Metrics-That-Matter

Now that we have outlined why an ERG measurement strategy is important and have reviewed key principles to keep in mind as they relate to metrics, let's explore some of the unique metrics that ERG track. The hope is that some of these will be adopted by a growing number of employee resource groups. The metrics are not listed in any particular order of importance but, rather, in a manner to convey a comprehensive set of metrics. Each of these metrics is actually captured by at least one existing ERG. It is also expected that in reviewing some of these metrics, ERGs might be able to create metrics that are not exactly the same, but similar. Either way, my goal in sharing these metrics is that it will elevate the measurement prowess of employee resource groups as a way to gauge their progress toward ERG excellence. Table 10.1 has the sample list of ERG metrics that matter.

Table 10.1 ERG Metrics-that-Matter 50 Most Commonly Used ERG Metrics

4C ERG Assessment	48-item assessment measures ERG performance across 4 dimensions – Careers, Community, Culture, and Commerce. Measures scores against a normative database of other ERGs. Allows ERGs to track progress.
Awards & Recognition	Track the number of external awards and recognitions received by the ERGs themselves or by individual ERG members. This is a Culture metric.
Benchmarking	Track number of ERGs that have participated in benchmarking activities and events with ERGs at other companies. This is a Community metric.
Business Unit Insights	Interactions with business units are tracked. Either business unit presentations to ERGs to increase business insight or ERG presentations to business units to increase awareness. This is a Commerce metric.
Bylaws & Role Descriptions	Firms keep track of how many of the ERGs have developed actual bylaws and how many of their ERG leadership roles have official role descriptions. This is a Culture metric.

(*Continued*)

Table 10.1 (*Continued*)

Chapters	Companies measure how many chapters each ERG has and then track growth in number of chapters year-over-year. This is a Culture metric.
Communication	ERGs count the number of newsletters, brochures, & marketing collateral they create to build ERG awareness. Several firms require a certain number of newsletters per year per ERG. This is a Culture metric.
Community Events & Attendance	Companies track the number of community events held by ERGs and ERG attendance at community events. This is a Community metric.
Community Influence	Companies track number of ERG members that serve on the board of directors or trustees of external community nonprofit and/or educational organizations as a way to grow ERG influence in a community. This is a Community metric.
Company Intranet	Usage of company ERG intranet is tracked to measure utilization of existing communication tools. This is a Culture metric.
Customer Feedback	Tracking of efforts where ERGs engage their members and external friends to test and provide feedback of company products & services from a diverse customer perspective. This is a Commerce metric.
Customer Referrals	Tracks efforts by ERG to refer new customers. For example, ERGs hand out coupons at events with unique code that can be tracked when redeemed by customers. This is a Commerce metric.
Customer Experience	List initiatives or support provided by ERG members to client/customer facing efforts (such as Hispanic ERG members providing bilingual translation support to client calls). This is a Commerce metric.

(*Continued*)

Table 10.1 (*Continued*)

Diversity Associations	Track the number of ERG members who are active members of external diversity associations such as the Society of Women Engineers and others. This is a Community metric.
Employee Engagement Survey	During companywide engagement survey, employees are asked if they are members of an ERG. Then they do an index to see if ERG members score higher in engagement on survey. This is a Culture metric.
Employee Giving	Encourage and track ERG member participation in internal company campaigns such as United Way contributions. This is a Commerce metric.
Employee Referrals	Track ERG member submissions to company employee referral program to measure impact on recruiting efforts. This is a Culture metric.
ERGs as Internal Consultants	Number of efforts led by ERGs to better educate and inform key internal functions about unique aspects related to their affinity. For example, sessions for recruiters on how to effectively interview and connect with job candidates who have a physical disability or are visually impaired. This is a Culture metric.
Event Attendance	Track how many people attend ERG events. Track year-over-year. This is a Community metric.
Executive Sponsor	Number of meetings ERG holds with their executive sponsor, D&I leader, or top HR executive are tracked to gauge alignment. This is a Commerce metric.
Exposure to Executives	Count the number of presentations given by top corporate executives to ERG members or number of meetings held with top executives to try to demonstrate increased exposure to top leaders. This is a Career metric.

(*Continued*)

Table 10.1 (*Continued*)

External Leadership Development	ERGs track the number of members who are asked to participate in external leadership development programs that are funded by the ERG or the organization. This is a Career metric.
External Partnerships	Track ERG involvement in helping firm select correct diverse external professional associations and nonprofits. Includes insights provided to HR, Community Affairs, Foundation, etc. This is a Community metric.
External Visibility	Track number of ERGs or ERG members who are profiled or highlighted in external magazines, newspapers, publications or who give presentations at conferences. This is a Commerce metric.
Funding	Metric that captures amount of money allocated to (or raised by ERG) to fund their network. Includes money provided by HR, diversity, or business units. This is a Culture metric.
Gov't Relations & Policy Impact	Tracking of efforts by ERGs to improve government relations and influence public policy. Examples include number of letters sent by ERG members to their local member of congress regarding key legislation. This is a Commerce metric.
High Potential	Track the number of ERG members that are part of a formal "High Potential" program or list created by the corporation. This is a Career metric.
Internal Customer Conversion	ERGs take an active role in promoting their company's products & services to their members as a way to drive sales. Internal customer efforts and resulting sales are tracked. This is a Commerce metric.
Member Profile	Polls conducted of ERG membership to determine profile, including average length of service, job level, location participation, duration of ERG involvement, etc. This is a Culture metric.

(*Continued*)

Table 10.1 (***Continued***)

Membership	Simple tracking of number of employees who are members of ERGs. Track year-over-year. This is a Culture metric.
Mentoring	Calculate the number of ERG members who are assigned a formal mentor. Track year-over-year. This is a Career metric.
Multicultural Marketing	List activities or support provided by ERGs to marketing department to gauge impact on multicultural or diversity marketing efforts by firm. This is a Commerce metric.
New Business Ideas	ERGs create formal initiative asking members to generate list of potential new products, cost-cutting efforts or new revenue generation concepts. Ideas are vetted and those implemented are tracked. This is a Commerce metric.
New Client Introductions	ERGs track introductions made by them to sales department for potential new clients. These business development introductions are track and resulting new business is tallied. This is a Commerce metric.
Onboarding	Track ERG efforts that help to onboard new employees to the organization, specifically those from historically underrepresented groups. Goal is to improve retention. This is a Culture metric.
Percentage of Workforce	Companies measure what percentage of their entire employee population is a member of an ERG then track membership over time. Goal is to target 8–10% as members. Often called Penetration Rate. This is a Culture metric.
Product Development	Track number of focus groups or formal input provided to new product development efforts to try to gauge input. This is a Commerce metric.

(*Continued*)

Table 10.1 (*Continued*)

Professional Development	Track number of ERG members who have taken internal professional development workshops and training modules. This is a Career metric.
Promotions	Annually calculate the number of ERG members who have been promoted. Compare to company average. Also known as promotional velocity. This is a Career metric.
Recruiting	Track number of ERG members who attended diversity recruiting events and expos as a representative of the company. This is a Culture metric.
Representation	List the numbers of locations, states, or countries that have ERG members. Measure expansion of reach & scope. This is a Culture metric.
Scholarships	Some ERGs raise money for scholarship purposes. Track amount of money raised year over year. This is a Community metric.
Social Media	ERGs establish Facebook, Twitter, or LinkedIn accounts and then track number of members, "Likes," followers, etc. This is a Commerce metric.
Sponsorship	Track number of ERG members who are formal participants in a company's sponsorship or executive development program. This is a Career metric.
Strategy Execution	End-of-year document that tracks performance against ERG goals established at the beginning of the year. Usually rated as "Met Goal/Did Not Meet Goal." This is a Culture metric.
Succession Planning	Determine how many ERG leadership positions have a "ready now" candidate to fill in once the current leader has left the role. This is a Culture metric.

(*Continued*)

Table 10.1 (*Continued*)

Supplier Diversity	Efforts to introduce new diverse suppliers and vendors by ERG are tracked. Measured in number of introductions made and money spent by company with diverse supplier. This is a Commerce metric.
Training Evaluation Scores	When ERG workshops are held, employees asked to rate the training. Measure average evaluation scores over time. This is a Career metric.
Turnover	Track number of ERG members who leave the organization. Compare the ERG member turnover rate versus the general turnover rate for employees. This is a Culture metric.
Volunteerism	ERGs ask employees to volunteer their time at community events and then sum the total numbers of volunteer hours by ERG members. This is a Community metric.

Along with data analytics, it is my belief the increased use of metrics will be a key component regarding the next generation of employee resource groups. The time for ERGs with a minimal or absent measurement strategy will soon be over. As this chapter outlines, ERGs can, and must, do better with regards to metrics if they are to achieve ERG excellence.

11 High Performers and High Potentials

ERGs and Talent Management

Traditionally, ERGs have been leveraged at leadership incubators with the perspective that senior organization leaders should serve as sponsors or advisors. Almost every organization treats ERGs as leadership incubators, providing junior staff the chance to flex talent muscles they might not have the opportunity to otherwise. The thinking is that if companies give ERG members access to professional development workshops and experience running a team and developing strategy, ERGs will build the next generation of group leaders.

However, once these ERG members begin to demonstrate their true leadership capability, they often leave the ERG. While helping to produce more leaders for the organization is still a valuable outcome, it does little to meet the growing leadership demands of the ERGs. Corporations also tend to assign senior leaders and executives to serve as ERG sponsors or advisors, rather than as leaders of these groups. This is not necessarily a bad decision, but often these busy individuals provide limited attention and support to the ERG. In many cases, the executive sponsor or advisor has never been an ERG member and thus has a limited perspective on what is needed to elevate performance.

But we are starting to see companies take on a new approach, one that has a focus on securing both junior- and senior-level employees as ERG leaders. Promoting from within an ERG helps to create a steady pipeline of future group leaders who have the visibility of, and access to, powers that be within the larger organization. This allows companies to identify and groom young, high-performing individuals for not only future ERG leadership roles, but also leadership positions across the broader organization. When done successfully, this serves to entice those outside of the ERG to become members. This approach requires a commitment to succession planning within ERGs and the overall organization so that employees serving as ERG leaders experience this role as a true steppingstone to more senior positions. This requires a tighter partnership with HR's well-established leadership development strategies and programs.

To be truly effective, this approach must be replicated, sustained, and scaled across all ERGs within an organization. And yet, employee groups that only serve as incubators for ERG and organization leaders are missing out on a key leadership resource. ERGs should also be open to leaders who have been nurtured in the formal parts of the organizations. Doing so requires corporations to include ERG leadership in their systematic leadership rotation programs.

Systematically bringing more senior leaders into the ERG immediately brings two benefits: their very presence and involvement serves as a magnet for other top performers and established leaders who already have the skills, savvy, and political capital necessary to make things happen within the organization. The ideal candidates for this strategy are those who have been deemed high performers and have the potential to become future executives within the corporation. Often, these individuals have reached the role of director and, in some cases, vice president. JPMorgan Chase, Bristol Myers Squibb, and

McDonald's Corporation are just a few of the companies that regularly have top business leaders and vice presidents at the head of their ERGs. ERGs that support women's initiatives seem to be the most effective in attracting senior leaders. Abbott Laboratories' Women Leaders in Action group, which is run by two senior-level women executive co-chairs, is just one example.

But before we begin delving deeper into tactics, let's look at how the alignment between ERGs and talent management is being built on a solid foundation. An analysis of data gathered from over 845 ERGs representing over 350 companies that are part of the 4C Assessment normative database indicates that as of Fall 2020, 58 percent of companies allow their ERGs to select and elect their own leaders, while 42 percent of these companies use an appointment process to determine ERG leaders. This indicates that more than half of all corporations still leverage an ERG election process in determining the leaders of their ERGs.

However, compared to a similar analysis conducted in 2014, the trend is clearly moving toward companies using an appointment process. In 2014, the analysis showed that only 30 percent of companies used an appointment process compared to the 42 percent that indicated they do so in 2020. This represents a 40 percent increase in the use of an appointment process and illustrates a paradigm shift in the way companies are looking at ERG leadership determination. This trend is further validated by recent interviews of chief diversity officers and ERG program managers who are increasingly viewing ERG leader appointments as their process of choice.

The ERG selection process is actively being reviewed and reexamined within corporate America, whether current ERG leaders like it or not. Of the companies that have transitioned to an ERG appointment process, most report being satisfied at having made the switch, even though they acknowledge that it is not an easy decision to make and that the transition process can be a difficult one.

You are likely asking yourself, "What is driving this shift toward an ERG appointment process, and is an appointment process the right one for my organization?" As ERGs have grown in sophistication and impact, companies' expectations for ERGs have risen, and so have the expectations of their leaders. While some companies are looking to enhance the amount of training and development given to existing ERG leaders, others are turning to an appointment process that many company executives believe will enhance the probability of the leaders' and ERG success. There are three common reasons why companies are looking to strengthen the leadership of ERGs.

First, the movement toward turning ERGs into business resource groups (BRGs) is significantly impacting the role of these groups within their company. At some companies, this name change may be a symbolic one. However, at many companies this evolution is quite substantial, moving away from the ERGs' more social nature toward networks that have a strong alignment with business goals. This requires not only a change in focus for the ERGs, but new capabilities in ERG leaders.

For example, Fifth Third Bank, a regional financial institution based in Cincinnati, Ohio, leverages their ERG leaders to participate in focus groups related to multicultural market initiatives. In order to effectively serve on these focus groups, their ERG leaders need a strong understanding of Fifth Third Bank's core financial offerings, client profile, community outreach initiatives, current employee demographics, customer contact experience, and cultural insights. Having a thorough understanding of the business has thus become a key qualification for employees who wish to lead their ERGs and to meet Fifth Third Bank's expectation that the groups support business initiatives.

Second, annual budgets allocated for ERGs have become quite large. In fact, there are many companies that have annual ERG budgets between $500,000 to $1 million a year. With such significant investments in their ERGs, companies need ERG leaders that have budget management experience and who have the business acumen to manage these funds accordingly.

Lastly, not all employees celebrate the growth in size and impact of ERGs. Some employees still see ERGs as being divisive in nature – the homogeneity of the membership viewed as exclusionary as opposed to inclusive. For this reason, some companies want to highlight the inclusive nature of ERGs by at times appointing leaders who are not from the particular affinity of the ERG.

These trends are requiring companies to examine the effectiveness of their ERG leader selection process and, for some, to at least consider if an ERG appointment process might be the best approach. Before making such a decision, however, companies are reviewing three key considerations in their determination of which ERG leader process to choose: ERG ownership, membership, and leadership development. These considerations serve as a useful starting place for companies as they examine the future of their ERG leader selection process.

ERG Ownership

Who is the perceived owner of ERGs at any company? At many organizations, ERGs are seen as grass roots entities that belong to employees. Employees perceive these networks as being for employees and therefore should be run by employees. At others, the ERGs have minimal input from the organization and, as such, it seems natural for the ERGs to want to determine and select their own leaders. This allows ERGs to select someone they feel is knowledgeable about the ERG and choose someone who has been actively involved for some time. ERGs often view the ability to select their own leader as a right they possess and one they value deeply. When this mentality exists within the ERG, efforts to change the selection process is viewed as a loss of control and an infringement by the company.

The ERGs at Allstate Insurance Company have existed since the mid-1980s and have always been a grassroots effort. Even back in 2006, when Allstate formalized its ERGs, it kept the spirit of grassroots efforts because Allstate learned that a high level of ERG engagement is critical for the long-term sustainability of their ERGs. According to Carlos Herrera, Allstate ERG program manager at the time, "Since all of our groups continue to thrive by grassroots efforts, we allow our ERG members to select their leader. Being chosen to lead an ERG by the membership is great recognition that should only be given to an individual whose followers have selected them. Allstate believes that ERG members know how to identify leaders who they want to follow and support, and we trust them to select who they believe is the best to serve in that role." Because of the approach at Allstate, any effort to switch toward an appointment model for their ERG leaders would go against the grassroots spirit they have held since their very inception.

Yet at other companies, it is clear that while the ERGs are run by employees, the ERGs are still sponsored and endorsed by the company. Because the ERGs are funded by the company, the company maintains ownership of the ERGs. As the owners of the ERGs, companies maintain the authority to choose who should lead them. In many cases, ERGs are viewed as any being similar to an official task force or standing committee at a company, and therefore the leaders should be appointed by the organization. In these organizations, executives would argue that leaders of the ERG should be identified using the same appointment approach.

Addressing the issue of perceived ownership of ERGs can be complicated, however, and companies should examine this subject thoroughly. It is true that companies fund the ERGs, but does that grant them ownership? Is that ownership transferred to the members if they are the ones running the ERG? Are ERGs to be viewed in the same manner as property in that ownership can be gained, lost, transferred, or exchanged? While comparing ERG ownership to the ownership of property may appear silly, the implications of this decision are anything but trivial. Companies will be well served in examine the issue of ownership from the perspective of multiple stakeholders before determining which point of view is best for them.

ERG Membership

ERGs are a resource for all employees at the entire organization, not just for those who are members of a certain constituency or affinity group. When ERG leaders are selected by their membership, the tendency is for them to select someone of that particular affinity with, for example, a woman running the women's ERG or a Latino running the Hispanic ERG. All ERGs should be inclusive and encourage employees from outside of a specific race, ethnicity, or affinity to join. This allows ERGs to have members who may not be a member of a specific affinity, but who are strong allies of that group.

Companies that favor the appointment approach like the additional freedom of being able to select a leader who is a strong ally but not necessarily someone with the same affinity or constituency as the ERG itself. Taking such an approach ensures that ERGs remain a resource not just for members of a constituency, but rather as a resource for all employees. Also, having an ERG leader not of that affinity further promotes the inclusive nature of ERGs.

If, however, a company wishes to appoint a leader of an ERG who is not of that affinity, this individual must possess a strong desire and willingness to lead the ERG. Toyia Rudd, former director of Talent Management & Inclusion at CDW, the integrated information technology solutions provider, says, "Consider only individuals with a passion for the ERGs purpose." Nothing will do more harm to the credibility of the appointment process, or to the appointed leader themselves, if they are not excited about, or strong advocates for, what ERGs do and their value to the organization.

ERGs are a very visual component of a company's diversity strategy. At some companies, ERGs serve as the "poster child" of a company's dedication to diversity and inclusion. The visibility and profile of ERG leaders can greatly shape perception and reputation of an ERG and, thus, of a company's commitment to diversity. Therefore, companies should think long and hard about what message they are sending to the broader employee population if all the members of an ERG are of the same race, gender, or affinity. Similarly, what is the message that is being sent to an ERG if someone not their affinity is appointed to lead their group? This simply goes to show that with great visibility comes great responsibility, and consequently, companies should consider the broader message they are sending based on the membership of their ERGs.

Leadership Development Mechanisms

Development plans for ERG leaders at many companies focus almost exclusively on their ERG responsibilities and only a small percentage of ERGs have formalized development plans for their ERG leaders. Those that do are not always aligned with a company's other leader development and talent management programs.

For example, the professional development activities for the ERGs at Kellogg's, the consumer-packaged goods company based in Battle Creek, Michigan, previously were separate initiatives run by each of their ERGs with little collaboration among the ERGs. While the sessions offered were often useful, they lack alignment with Kellogg's broader business strategy and diversity goals. When Kellogg's made the decision to transition to an appointment process for their ERG leaders, part of the decision involved being able to better align the development of their ERG leaders with their broader development initiatives.

Cigna, the health insurance company, appoints the leaders of their colleague resource groups. Cigna's chief diversity officer indicates that one of the considerations for the appointment process was to ensure that the ERGs did not establish development processes that had competing infrastructure. By appointing the leaders of their colleague resource groups, Cigna aligns the development of ERG leaders to their talent review process and found it to be a more organized way to connect these groups with our talent planning process.

The ability to develop talent effectively is an important aspect of a company's human capital strategy. As such, an ERGs level of responsibility in grooming and developing future leaders should always be a key aspect of their value proposition to not only the organization, but to their members as well. Thus, the effectiveness of an ERG to develop leaders should always be assessed and reviewed periodically and ultimately should weigh heavily in any decision related to the selection process for ERG leadership.

ERG Leader Competencies

Regardless of whether an ERG leader is elected by the membership or appointed by the company, companies are taking steps to ensure that these leaders are well prepared to lead. Below are the common characteristics being used by companies in determining their leaders. If these capabilities and qualities are found consistently in ERG leaders selected by the membership, then this may diminish the need to transition to an appointment process. If these attributes are not found consistently in your ERG leaders, then movement to an appointment process should receive high consideration.

High Performance

ERG leaders must have demonstrated an ability to perform their jobs with distinction. This means they have a history of consistently meeting and surpassing the workplace goals that have been established for them. High performers also tend to be good at managing their time and workload. This is critical for leaders of an ERG because their ERG workload is often above and beyond their existing job.

High performers also tend to perform well with a great deal of autonomy. Because ERG leaders are not closely monitored by an immediate supervisor when performing their ERG activities, the ability to work well autonomously is often critical to their success. When ERG leadership roles are filled with strong performers, it sends the rest of the company a message that the ERG is serious about making a big impact.

Business Credibility

Deborah Elam, former chief diversity officer for General Electric, stated, "If the leaders of the ERGs are not credible with business executives, then the ERG will not be credible." When ERG leaders are individuals who consistently and significantly outperform their peers in the workplace, they develop credibility. That means they have built trust and confidence among colleagues, executives, and a wide array of internal and external stakeholders.

Because GE uses an appointment process for the leaders of their ERGs, the company is able to appoint those who are not only credible but who are also highly influential.

Business credibility is also established when an ERG leader possesses strong business acumen, including the knowledge and understanding of financial, accounting, marketing, and operational functions of an organization. Along with their business literacy, credibility is further conveyed through their acute perception of the dimensions of business issues through thoughtful analysis of business decisions.

Strategic Mindset

Effective ERG leaders are also those who understand that organizations are an ecosystem that requires balance to operate effectively. When they possess this understanding, they are better equipped to view ERGs as being a part of a bigger picture. This strategic mindset allows them to understand the needs of colleagues, stakeholders, and the organization as a holistic system and they incorporate these points of view into their ERG planning.

Strategically minded ERG leaders also continuously scan their organization to identify ERG value-creation opportunities and synergistic collaborations across departments. This demonstrates respect and consideration for others' agendas and work outcomes in ways that result in being viewed as a reliable business partner. If ERG leaders do not possess a strategic mindset, they are more apt to demonstrate self-serving tendencies when pressing for ERG priorities.

Ability to Develop Others

In order for organizations to have ERGs that are sustainable over a long period of time, it is not enough to have strong leaders at the top. Rather, it is essential that these leaders build leadership capability throughout the ERG to ensure the future success of the group after the current leader moves on. Not only does this serve an ERG well, but it also has the potential to provide an organization with a diverse pool of well-developed talent for future advancement.

Building Effective Teams

Strong ERG leaders create and run highly effective leadership teams. These ERG leaders realize that even good intentions and a great effort will not get an ERG very far if the leadership team is doing the wrong things well or the right things wrong. They focus on the things that help promote effective teams – such as clarity, precision, and attention to detail when it comes to roles, responsibilities, and expectations. These ERG leaders are able to instill a "we versus me" mindset within the group. They demonstrate to others that in order to build trust, one must be reliable and dependable.

ERG leaders who can build effective teams are often able to avoid common ERG team derailers. For example, they are successful in avoiding cliques and they quickly eliminate any power shifts, turf battles, and infighting issues. They also avoid grapevine and gossip issues by keeping clear lines of communication within the ERG. Finally, they effectively navigate the issues that arise when peers manage peers within the ERG.

Transitioning to an Appointment Process

Once companies have reviewed the key considerations and leadership qualities outlined previously, they should be in a good position to determine what ERG selection process is best for them. If the decision is made to transition from election to appointment of ERG leaders, this process should not be taken lightly. It will serve a company well to utilize a change management approach when handling the transition process. Below are key components that companies should incorporate into their transition process from election to appointment of ERG leaders.

Current ERG Leader Input – The ERG leaders currently in place, because of the previous election process, will most likely not be particularly excited about the decision to transition to an appointment process. They may feel that the new process takes away their control over the ERG and see it as a signal that they are not doing a sufficient job. One step some companies have taken to avoid these perceptions is to ask current ERG leaders what the criteria for appointing ERG leaders should be. When they were considering transitioning to an appointment process, Northwestern Mutual, the insurance and financial services company based in Milwaukee, Wisconsin, asked the leadership teams of their current ERGs to help define the requirements of future ERG leaders. In addition, each ERG gave their own point of view regarding whether future ERG leaders should be of the same affinity. Northwestern Mutual solicited similar input from their ERG leaders on other topics such as job level requirements, previous ERG experience, and specific competencies. This input was collected by members of the Northwestern Mutual diversity and inclusion team and was used in helping to finalize the decision of how their future ERG leaders were to be identified. By soliciting the input of their current ERG leaders, Northwestern Mutual helped gain their buy-in, regardless of the decision they make.

Executive Sponsor Buy-In

Executive sponsors play a key role in guiding ERGs and advocating on their behalf. Therefore, their input on whether or not to transition to an appointment process is essential, and they will need to continue to be engaged throughout the transition process itself.

Since executive sponsors serve as champions for ERGs, they must also champion the decision to move toward an appointment process. They must clearly articulate to their ERGs and the rest of the organization that appointing ERG leaders aligns with the direction that the company is taking with their ERGs. Through their communication and their visibility on the subject, there should be no doubt that executive sponsors' support is critical to ERGs going through this transition.

Executive sponsors should also play an active role in helping to define the criteria that should be used to appoint new ERG leaders. Their advice and counsel should guide the identification and selection of the appointed leaders. In addition, executive sponsors can serve as talent scouts for the ERG leader positions, playing a crucial role in identifying candidates that should be considered for the ERG leader roles.

Communicating the Reason for Change

Because transitioning to an appointment process is a significant undertaking, organizations should move slowly and deliberately. This includes being clear to employees as to why the change is being made. In early 2014, Johnson Controls, a global diversity technology firm, began informing employees that it planned to transition to an ERG leader appointment process. Their director of global workforce diversity at Johnson Controls, stated, "Companies should start by saying that the change is an effort to vet the candidates that are being considered so that the best employees run the business resource groups." Next, Johnson Controls held a two-day BRG leadership summit that included training for the BRG executive sponsors on how they could be stronger advocates for the BRGs and their role in the appointment transition. The summit also included a panel with leaders from other companies that have ERG appointment processes so that employees could ask questions about how their process worked and the benefits of such an approach.

Alignment with Talent Management

Organizations that choose to have their ERG leaders appointed have the added flexibility of being able to connect their ERG leadership roles with their other talent management efforts. For example, those whom the company have deemed as being high potentials can now be selected to run an ERG as part of their development process. An ERG leadership role can give someone, who the company has deemed as high potential, valuable experiences such as leading a team, managing a budget, setting a strategy, aligning with business, community outreach, and an opportunity to strengthen their cultural competence. For those who have already proven their leadership abilities, appointment processes allow a company to place a strong performer in an ERG leader role to help strengthen an ERG that may be in need of a boost.

ERG leader appointment also allows a company to place someone who is in need of increased visibility in a role that enhances their exposure across the enterprise. In doing so, the company is leveraging the ERG leadership role as a vehicle not only to groom future leaders, but also as a vehicle to expand their network and profile. Especially when leadership opportunities are limited, companies must place disproportionate attention on developing the people they think will lead their ERGs, and the organization, into the future. Having an appointment process prevents ERG leadership roles from becoming an underutilized asset.

The examination of the process by which companies identify their ERG leaders is evidence of the growing significance ERGs play in corporate America. If ERG impact were insignificant, interest in who is leading them would be minimal. However, as ERG influence has grown, and the challenges they have been asked to confront has risen, companies are being forced to reevaluate their traditional approaches to ERG leader identification. It is no longer acceptable for companies to assume that past leader selection processes are still relevant in this new age of next-generation ERGs. Companies have an obligation to ensure their governance practices are still viable even as shifts in ERG focus, funding, and inclusivity have occurred.

But changing the ERG leader selection process requires audacity and thoroughness because of the considerable implications and somewhat emotional aspects of leader selection. It is critical that companies review their ERG leader process using the lens of ownership, membership, and leadership development at the very minimum. Additionally, the required competence and abilities of ERG leaders dictates that companies examine and test their assumptions about what selection process is best for them.

Those that use an appointment process appear to feel that this approach allows them to elevate the power and influence of their ERGs while at the same time giving the company more jurisdiction over the ERGs. But most importantly, those that use the appointment process tend to feel that the ability to place high-performing individuals, of their choosing, in ERG leader roles provides a clear payoff.

But even though a growing number of companies are moving toward the appointment approach, it does not mean that this approach works for every organization. Nor is the trend toward an appointment process an indictment that allowing ERG members to elect their own leaders is an outdated or ineffective approach. In fact, there are just as many, if not more, high-performing ERGs that allow their ERG members to elect their own leaders than there are those that appoint their leaders.

For now, the only real conclusion that can be made is that the ERG leader selection process is a critical component in determining the ultimate success of ERGs. It is hard to argue that having stronger ERG leaders results in having stronger ERGs. So as ERGs grow in impact and influence, those that have the strongest leaders will reap the greatest rewards. The competitive advantage will thus reside in those companies that use process that best determines who those ERG leaders will be.

Organizations that have an appointment process have three distinct benefits. First, the performance of their ERGs tends to be very high. This high performance is a direct result of having leaders with high capability and advanced skill sets. For example, at Cigna, the appointment of the leaders for their Lesbian, Gay, Bi-Sexual, Transgender and Allies Colleague Resource Group has allowed them to raise awareness of issues for their LGBTQ employees and has helped Cigna provide even more culturally competent care to the gay community. The LGBTA Colleague Resource Group has also played a key role in helping Cigna in the past achieve a perfect score of 100 on the Human Rights Campaign Corporate Equality Index.

Second, the appointed leaders tend to serve as magnets for other high performers. When employees see ERGs being run by those deemed to be of high potential and with a history of high performance, the ERGs are perceived in a more positive light. Because the ERGs are held in higher regard, more employees want to be involved. Involvement in the ERGs at General Electric (GE) by senior leaders is quite significant and membership has grown because of the reputation of the appointed leaders of their ERGs. Engagement of high performers and senior leaders in the ERGs at GE is also demonstrated by reviewing the talent pool it uses to appoint the leaders of their ERG. Every year, GE identifies its top leaders based on individual performance, achievement of business results, and future potential. Anyone appointed to run one of GE's ERGs must come from this group of the company's top leaders, thus ensuring active engagement in their ERGs by proven leaders.

Third, having an appointment process tends to diminish resistance of ERGs by middle managers who previously did not see the true value of the resource groups. Resistance is diminished not only because of the higher level of performance by the ERGs and their larger membership, but because of the reputation of the appointed leaders.

For example, the Women's Network Leader at GE was recently tasked with inviting an executive at GE to speak at a local event in Louisville, Kentucky. The leader of the Women's Network briefed the executive about the speaking opportunity, highlighted the benefits to GE if the executive accepted the invitation, and was able to influence the executive to speak at the event. The credibility of the Women's Network leader with business executives allowed her to accomplish the task of securing a guest speaker. Without an appointment process that ensures ERG leaders have credibility, it may have been more difficult for the Women's Network Leader to secure a meeting with a business unit executive to brief them about an external speaking opportunity.

In my experience in working with ERGs, two things have become very clear to me. First, ERGs only tend to be as strong as their leaders. It is difficult to reach ERG excellence without having talented individuals leading the group and helping to chart the course. The second aspect is that too often, the demand for strong ERG leaders exceeds the supply. That might sound a bit harsh, particularly given the deep amount of respect that I have for ERG leaders. But in reality, ERGs need leaders who are not only passionate and well-liked but also talented and capable of providing strong leadership.

The acknowledgment that strong leaders are critical to the success of ERGs is the driving force as to why more and more companies are aligning their ERGs with talent management initiatives. In 2019, I was involved in a consulting engagement with Verizon, the telecommunications company, regarding the ERG leader selection process. I needed more information about the connection between ERGs and talent management, so I initiated a research study of 40 organizations from a variety of industries (see Table 11.1).

Table 11.1 ERG and Talent Management Study List of 40 Participating Companies

Abbott Laboratories	Akamai Technologies
Biogen	Boeing
CapitalOne	Dell Computers
Dow Chemical	Eli Lilly
Facebook	General Electric
General Motors	Groupon
Harley Davidson Motorcycles	Health Care Service Corporation
Herman Miller	Intel Corporation
KraftHeinz	Liberty Mutual Insurance
MassMutual	McDonald's Corporation
MetLife	MillerCoors
National Grid	Nielsen
Nike	Northern Trust
Northwestern Mutual	Pacific Gas & Electric
PepsiCo	Progressive Insurance
Prudential Insurance	RR Donnelley & Sons
SC Johnson	Shell Oil
Spectrum Health	State Street Corporation
Travelers Insurance	Uber
VMware	Walgreens

The results were fascinating and verified my assumption regarding ERGs and talent management. First, 60 percent of the companies in the study appointed their ERG leaders as opposed to having them elected by the membership. Even among those that did use an election process, over one-third (36 percent) planned to move toward an appointment process. Second, the majority of companies indicated that they were moving toward an appointment process because they wanted greater oversight regarding who would be leading their ERGs. Not only did they want oversight, but they also wanted the ability to place individuals who were considered high performers and high potentials into the ERG leader roles. By doing so, not only did they help to ensure strong leaders at the top of their ERGs, they also were leveraging the ERG leader role as a developmental experience for top performers. This is a sign of a company striving for ERG excellence. Table 11.2 highlights the top five findings from the ERG and Talent Management research study.

Table 11.2 Summary of Top 5 Findings ERGs and Talent Management Study

1. Companies are moving toward greater alignment between ERG leader roles and their talent management processes.
2. Alignment with talent management allows companies to top-grade, or elevate, the caliber of leaders running their ERGs.
3. The alignment with talent management actually makes the ERG leader role more highly desired by high potentials and high performers.
4. The ERG leader role thus becomes a mechanism to groom future leaders and a destination for existing leaders.
5. Alignment with talent management mitigates the risk that ERG leaders are simply in those roles because they are well liked, popular, or because no one else really wanted the role.

An interesting observation did arise when connecting with the companies that were included in the study. Several mentioned that at one point, the ERG leader roles were not highly desired. Numerous companies indicated situations within their ERGs where the leader was in place because no one else really wanted the role. In these situations, the ERGs had a leader but often someone who was not particularly enthused about being in the role. These same companies indicated, however, that once they transitioned to an appointment process and ERGs could see that there was much more thought and consideration put into the ERG leadership role, interest in the same ERG leader role increased, whereas before the transition to an appointment process, interest in the role was not too significant.

One company that may be charting the course with regards to alignment between ERGs and talent management is Bristol Myers Squibb, the American multinational pharmaceutical company headquartered in New York City. At Bristol Myers Squibb, the leaders of their People and Business Resource Groups (PBRGs) report directly to members of the company's leadership team and act as an advisory group on key business initiatives related to diversity and inclusion. The PBRG leaders, called global leads, have dedicated full-time roles and are charged with developing multiyear plans that include business strategy, execution, and financial plans; membership growth and engagement; as well as the accelerated leadership development of its constituency base.

The approach used by Bristol Myers Squibb also includes leadership team accountability. Functioning as the board of directors for each PBRG, senior leaders are accountable for the governance of each PBRG as well as the career development of the full-time global leads. Business performance and governance is also a key component to the Bristol Myers Squibb approach as each PBRG business plan is linked to the company strategy and objectives with performance oversight by the Bristol Myers Squibb Leadership Team and the Global

Diversity and Inclusion Council. This empowers employee members to drive value and leverage their scientific and patient expertise, talent connections, and community partnerships to meet the needs of the company's diverse patient base.

The key component in the Bristol Myers Squibb approach is their departure from how every other company handles the leaders of their ERGs. To my knowledge, Bristol Myers Squibb is the only company in the world whose ERG leaders serve in that capacity as their full-time job. Each of the global leads for the company's eight People and Business Resource Group is already a top performer who has been deemed to have high potential. But by making their roles full-time jobs, the company is making a strategic investment not only financially but also operationally by having the most direct alignment between ERG leader roles and talent management. In my opinion, this is a clear sign of ERG excellence. And by highlighting this practice in this book, hopefully more will follow the example set by Bristol Myers Squibb and consider making their ERG leadership roles full-time positions.

12 Strategic Planning

Using the Google Maps Approach

Who doesn't love the Google Maps app? You know, the one many of us use to figure out how to get from where we are to where we want to go. This web mapping application is so popular that at one point not long ago it was determined that it was the world's most popular smartphone app. If you are not familiar with Google Maps, the application uses a global positioning system (GPS) to provide turn-by-turn navigation that allows someone to get from one point to another by following directions using a specific route.

How Google Maps works is simple. A person simply uses their computer, car, or smartphone and first indicates their current exact location, usually indicated by a blue dot on the device, followed by the desired destination, either by entering an address or selecting a location on the application. Then the application calculates several routes that allow the user to get from where they are to where they want to go. Some routes might be the fastest, some routes may be the shortest, or some might be the most scenic. The user can also indicate if they are driving, walking, or taking public transportation, and the map will determine the best route. Also, as someone starts toward their destination, the application provides updates based on traffic or road conditions. It simply is an amazing application.

As ERGs embark on their journey toward excellence, they should use the Google Maps approach when it comes to strategic planning. My friend Angel Gomez recommended that I use the Google Map analogy as it relates to strategic planning. Simply put, ERGs should first determine where they are (current state), articulate where they want to go (future state), and then chart a course to get their ERG from point A to point B. Sounds simple enough, but in my experience, many ERGs do not take an approach similar to the approach used by the Google Maps application. Too often, ERGs just start planning random events and activities that may sound appealing or interesting, but there is no rhyme or reason to their strategic plan. Sure, the ERG may be doing things, but their plan is ad hoc, splintered, or lacking direction. It is as if the ERG is going out on a Sunday drive, so it doesn't really need Google Maps because there is no starting point, ending point, or desired route.

The diversity and inclusion departments often contribute to poor strategic planning by ERGs. Typically, D&I departments will ask their ERGs to submit an annual business plan of initiatives and events that they plan to hold in the upcoming year. D&I then often uses these plans to help determine budget resources for the ERGs. The problem is that D&I professionals do not often ask their ERGs to determine their current state before creating a plan. Nor do they ever ask ERGs to outline their desired future state. They just want their list of upcoming events and initiatives. It is no wonder that ERGs often do not use the Google Maps approach to strategic planning; it is because they are not advised to by their D&I partners.

Other times, the ERG may indeed have a purpose or goal in mind, a desired future state. They then start charting a course and putting in plans to achieve that goal. But without any knowledge of where the ERG is at the moment, or their current state, it is almost impossible for them to know if their goals are realistic or how long it may take to achieve their goals. This is usually the most common mistake ERGs make when it comes to strategic planning.

And even if an employee resource group has both a desired future state and a clear idea of their current state, they still may embark on plans and initiatives that don't get them from where they are to where they want to go. Resources may not be sufficient, ERG leaders could change, other priorities could come up, and a variety of other elements could arise that may hinder their strategic plan. So as ERGs strive toward achieving excellence, here is the Google Map approach for strategic planning.

First, Determine ERG Current State

Before an employee resource group starts putting together a strategic plan, it must first gain an accurate perspective as to its current health and status. An ERG needs to have a general understanding of their state of wellbeing so that it is enabled to take a proactive step toward excellence and to mitigate the risk posed by common derailers. The results of any sort of assessment or analysis of an ERG's current state provide critical information in shaping a strategic plan. The 4C Assessment, ERG metrics, benchmarking, and SWOT analysis are recommended tools to help an ERG determine their current state.

Figure 12.1 shows a SWOT analysis conducted by an ERG to determine their current state.

The most effective and accurate method for determining an ERGs current state is the 4C Assessment (see Chapter 9). The 4C Assessment allows ERG members themselves to share how they feel the employee resource group is performing. This eliminates anecdotal guessing as to what is and is not working for employee resource groups. Members are in the best position to identify areas of strength as well as identify areas of concern for the ERG. Since the 4C Assessment asks members to evaluate the ERG across each of the 4C pillars, it also provides a comprehensive examination of the group's current state.

Since the 4C Assessment also allows various cuts of the data (by location, by ERG role, by job level, or by business unit, for example),

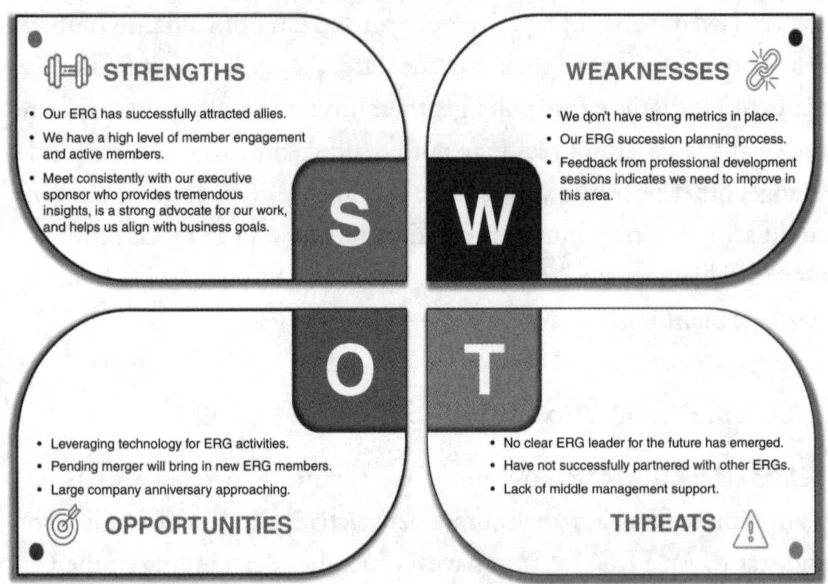

Figure 12.1 ERG SWOT Analysis: Current State Determination

an ERG gains insight that are more granular and useful. For example, in early 2021, I worked with an organization based out of Silicon Valley that runs a professional online networking platform. They conducted the 4C Assessment™ to gauge the current state of their ERGs. One insight gained was that the assessment scores for ERG members located in North America and Latin America were much higher than the assessment scores for ERG members located in their Asia Pacific (APAC), Europe, Middle East, and African (EMEA) regions. This was useful insight for all the ERGs because the 4C Assessment identified a previously unknown area of concern. With the data-driven insights, the ERGs now had a more accurate picture of their current state and could use this data in forming their strategic plan.

State Street Corporation, the financial services firm based in Boston, Massachussets, conducts the 4C Assessment approximately every two years. This allows the firm to consistently understand the current state of their ERGs. The assessment results are used so that the ERGs can make more data-driven decisions regarding their strategic plans. A recent 4C Assessment indicated that the ERGs were exceptionally strong when it comes to collaboration. Since collaboration was an area of strength for the ERGs, the ERGs outlined several areas of collaboration with each other in their strategic plans. The assessment also pointed out that members wanted stronger professional development offerings from their ERGs. Again, the ERGs were able to use these insights from the assessment to gauge their current state and use this information in their strategic planning process.

If an employee resource group has a strong measurement strategy, metrics can also be instrumental in determining the ERG's current state. An ERG metric is a quantifiable measurement of some aspect of performance for the employee resource group. Some ERGs call these metrics key performance indicators, or KPIs. ERGs can use metrics and KPIs in just about any aspect of their ERG (see Chapter 10). When an ERG captures various metrics, these metrics can be put into some sort of scorecard or dashboard that allows the ERG to constantly know how it is performing. Not only do metrics identify areas that need ERG attention, but they also provide an opportunity for the ERG to consider how it will respond.

For example, the ERGs of a large retailer track a metric that indicates how many of their current eight ERGs have a successor identified for the chair role. This allows the ERGs to constantly know if they have someone who is "ready now" to assume the chair role. If the number of ready candidates is low, the ERGs adjust their strategic plans accordingly by making succession planning and leadership continuity a priority. When the number of ready-now candidates is steady or high, they know that succession planning does not need to be included in their upcoming strategic plans. By tracking the metric of ERG chair succession, this employee resource group is able to consistently monitor their current state related to this area of performance.

Next, Establish a Desired Future State

The future is on its way, whether we like it or not or whether we are prepared for it or not. Regardless of whether an ERG thinks of the future as next year or some longer time horizon, hopefully the employee resource group has a vision for the future state of their ERG. When trying to determine a desired future state for an ERG, try to take into consideration an external scan of the environment. What are some of the primary trends impacting the members of your ERG? How is the company planning to leverage ERGs in the future?

Once this is done, ERGs should start brainstorming about potential future-state scenarios. At this stage, don't try to determine how viable it might be to achieve, but rather, think about possible scenarios. Soon, an ERG will want to begin thinking about criteria it will use to determine future state scenarios that might be achievable. This is when you start to think about your current state analysis. Potential criteria could be membership size, leadership succession, measurement results, and so on. Eventually, the ERG will want to choose a desired future by determining which potential future-state scenarios are most possible and feasible. Finally, you'll want to decide on the desired future state of your ERG.

This might sound easy, but it is not. A few things to consider along the way:

- You will want to state your desired future state in the future tense.
- Your future state needs to inspire by balancing two parts "aspiration" and one part "achievability."
- The ERG needs to be stretched and also simultaneously believe the future state is possible to achieve.
- The ERG should next try to develop a one- or two-line future vision statement. This allows the ERG to create something memorable. You'll know when your desired future state is memorable when other ERG members start repeating it.

Let me describe a recent client engagement to illustrate how this process works. In February 2021, Ingredion Inc., a multinational ingredient provider, asked me to work with its Hispanic ERG to help them shape their desired future state. In my first meeting with the Hispanic ERG leadership team, I described that their envisioned future should convey something visible, vivid, and real. Next, we reviewed future state examples of Latino ERGs from other companies:

- Become a BRG whose members are comfortable being unapologetically Latino.
- Become the BRG most known for helping the company nurture Latino employee success.
- Become the most powerful and inclusive BRG at the company.
- Push the company to have an increasingly Latino identity.
- Alleviate the stigma associated with being Hispanic so that Latinos see their ethnicity as an asset and source of strength.
- Become the BRG best known for helping its members bring their full selves to work.

Next, we started brainstorming ideas for potential future-state scenarios and ultimately landed on two potential future state scenarios:

1. To be sought out by Ingredion as internal advisors on Latino culture and heritage as well as by Hispanics globally who desire greater representation of Latinos and Latinas in leadership roles.
2. To build bridges of understanding that lead to greater acceptance of Hispanics so that Ingredion can more effectively tap into the many assets that Latinos and Latinas bring to the workplace.

Ultimately, the Latino ERG at Ingredion decided to go with statement number one as their desired future state. Now that the Latino ERG at Ingredion had both a current state and a desired future state, it could then begin creating their strategic plan using these two frames of reference and the Google Maps analogy as their guide. This is also the process I recommend that ERGs follow as they create their strategic plans. In my opinion, employee resource groups should determine their current state on an annual or biannual basis. With regards to future state scenarios, my recommendation would be to revisit these every three to four years.

Finalize Your Strategic Plan

The ERG strategic plan will empower members to set specific objectives and milestones that will help them strive towards their desired future state. The strategic plan for an ERG should define what critical to achieve over the next year to progress toward longer-term targets as well provide a mechanism to keep the ERG accountable for reaching stated goals. A well-formulated strategic plan also keeps the ERG members united and focused, energizing them to be more productive. Not only does a robust strategic plan provide an ERG with a stronger connection to their desired future state, but it also puts their ERG mission into daily practice. Equally important, the strategic plan provides ERG members with a clear sense of direction.

In short, the ERG strategic plan provides the nuts and bolts of the necessary work to be done over the coming year or performance cycle.

A good ERG strategic plan should include these common elements. First, a listing of key initiatives or events the ERG plans to undertake within the next year. As stated before, these initiatives should be well thought out with regards to helping to get the ERG from their current state to their desired future state. Next, someone from the ERG should be assigned as being responsible for the successful implementation or completion of these key tasks, initiatives, or events. This will help promote accountability for the successful execution of the ERG strategic plan.

Budget requirements should also be listed. This will help the ERG determine if it has the financial resources necessary for each of the key initiatives. These projections will help the ERG to anticipate budgetary outlays as well as costs to be incurred. Timelines and checkpoints are also recommended so that the ERG can keep track of progress. Of course, metrics or KPIs should be included that will indicate how successful you've been in achieving ERG goals. Once completed, the ERG strategic plan becomes clear. When the entire process comes together, ERG members can plainly see how it will achieve a desired future state. Ideas now become actions. Table 12.1 shows an example of a relatively straightforward annual ERG strategic plan.

Some ERG strategic plans include a longer time horizon and break down key objectives done into yearly components. Figure 12.2 is an example of a five-year ERG strategic plan that clearly outlines the

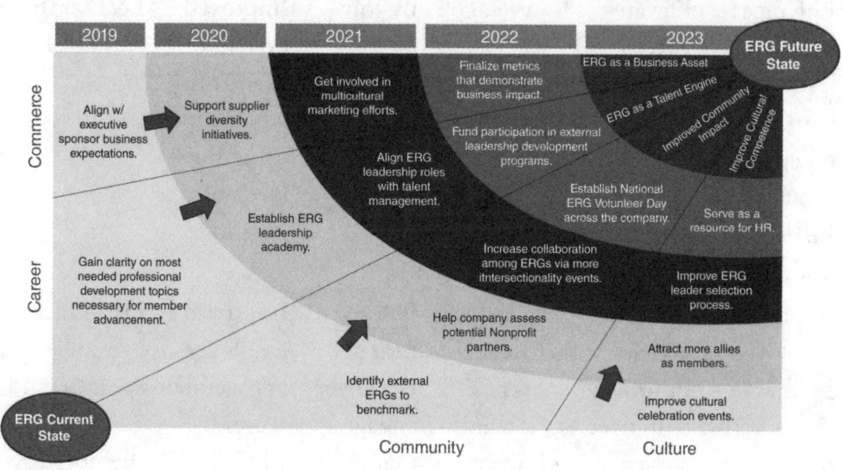

Figure 12.2 ERG Strategic Five-Year Plan

Table 12.1 ERG Strategic Planning 1-Year Plan

Business drivers (company and/or local)	ERG initiative	Link to ERG future state	Time frames	Measures of success	Key stakeholders
Increase % of employees who own company stock.	Launch ESOP drive within ERG.	Better align ERG with business initiatives.	By end of Q2 2020	# of new employees who now own company stock.	Human Resources and Employee Benefits Department.
Reduce # of community nonprofits supported locally.	Select key nonprofit partner per ERG chapter location.	Stronger community influence and impact.	By end of Q3 2020	Increased amount of funding provided to single nonprofit partner.	Community Affairs, Company Foundation and D&I.
Enhance quality of leadership workshop offerings provided to ERG leaders.	Elevate ERG member leadership capability and skill attainment.	Leverage leadership workshop to improve ERG member activity.	By July 2020	Improved evaluation scores of workshops using the 4 levels of learning.	L&D, HR, and D&I.
Improve employee survey scores across the enterprise.	Link ERG activity with improved employee survey scores.	Increase ERG value proposition and impact.	Before next all-employee engagement survey in Q4 2020.	Improved employee engagement scores by ERG members.	HR, D&I, executive sponsor, and ERG members.

employee resource current state, the desired future state, and how the ERG plans to reach this desired future state within five years.

Ultimately, each organization and employee resource group will have to determine which ERG strategic plan template or time horizon works best for them. The goal, however, is to enhance the strategic planning proficiency within ERGs so they can have a clearer line of sight as to how they will reach their objectives and desired future state.

13 Next-Generation ERGs

The ERG Excellence Manifesto

ERGs are indeed at a crossroads. They are either ascending in their prominence or their relevancy is being questioned. In either case, employee resource groups and the companies they operate within must confront the challenges outlined throughout this book. In doing so, ERGs need to be ready for new ways of thinking and operating that may be counter to long-cherished notions of what makes employee resource groups tick.

This will require courage and effective leadership. Companies also need to reevaluate their views of ERGs. It's puzzling how some organizations don't aggressively support their employee resource groups even while many of their senior leaders recognize that diversity provides a competitive advantage. It's organizationally inconsistent when some ERG activities are undermined by management at a time when leadership rhetoric seems focused on engagement and retention and more open lines of communication.

Employee resource groups are brimming with the potential to provide collaborative breakthroughs that build competency among its members, rather than dependency. Because of the competitive nature of business today, organizations cannot afford to operate in a manner that prevents ERG members from being heard. If this happens, organizations miss potential contributions, innovations, solutions, and creativity of these valuable employees. Companies and ERGs that embrace the new approaches presented here will go a long way in reaping the benefits of strong, vibrant employee resource groups.

The resiliency that employee resource groups have demonstrated throughout the pandemic has been both difficult and satisfying to watch. On the challenging side, seeing some employee resource groups lose the momentum that they worked so hard to establish was frustrating to see. It pained me to see the many 2020 ERG calendars full of promising initiatives be scrapped as the pandemic made their planned initiatives obsolete or simply too difficult to hold. Throughout the year of 2020, I was saddened to hear of the various ERG leaders and members who were no longer with their organizations due to their roles being eliminated or because they had to reluctantly leave their jobs in order to care for their children or their parents. I would get discouraged each time a diversity and inclusion practitioner informed me that they had to cut the budgets for their employee resource groups because their own D&I budgets were cut. It pained me to see once-active ERG members have to pull back so they could concentrate more fully on their day jobs because they were now doing the job of two people due to staff reductions.

It was also disturbing to see many ERG leaders cut their leadership terms short because they simply couldn't handle running an ERG under this new work environment. I felt compassion when I heard the ERG members were requesting their employee resource groups to hold workshops on anxiety, depression, mental health, dealing with difficult employees, and overall well-being. My heart went out to the ERG members who, during ERG Zoom call meetings, would tell their fellow ERG members they missed seeing them in person. And I was not surprised to see the drop in 4C ERG Assessment scores because so many employee resource groups were in a state of transition.

But then, almost simultaneously, I would feel a sense of satisfaction when I would see ERG leaders apply some of the new skills they had learned through my ERG leadership development workshops. I felt a sense of pride when I saw Black ERGs step up and hold amazing events in support of the Black Lives Matter movement and in response to the George Floyd murder. A sense of fulfillment filled my soul as I saw the other ERGs show their support for the Black community by publicly proclaiming their allyship. It was rewarding to see employee resource groups rally around their local organizations and national nonprofits as they elevated their community outreach efforts. I was amazed to see the heightened level of collaboration among the ERGs as they vowed to get through the difficult pandemic together. It was heartwarming to see ERG members genuinely show compassion and support for each other as we all struggled through this difficult time together, considering that many of us were almost paralyzed by the fear of the virus or grieving the loss of a loved one due to the pandemic.

An analysis of the results from 4C Assessments completed since the beginning of 2020 shows that employees have gained a sense of belonging. Some of that is based on an increased focus on allyship and on a higher level of comfort related to their sense of identity in the workplace and full embrace of intersectionality. Results also indicated stronger scores in the Community pillar as ERGs focused on building and maintaining a sense of community with their coworkers, even though they couldn't see them in person on a daily basis like before.

I also saw many employee resource groups revisit their core mission or refine their desired future state for the ERGs based on all the changes brought by the Covid-19 pandemic. As old ERG strategic plans were made obsolete, new ones were quickly developed. This is partly due to the enhanced capability in ERG strategic planning that has been improving over the last several years.

Personally, I found a silver lining resulting from the Covid-19 pandemic, and that was a drastic change to my business model. Prior to the pandemic, the default was to hop on a plane and travel to wherever my client was located to deliver a keynote speech, facilitate an ERG leadership workshop, or to simply provide consulting services. The result was a schedule that had me traveling about once a week all over the country. Those who travel know that life on the road is difficult on one's physical health, emotional well-being, and family life. The silver lining was that my consulting business had the best year financially in 2020 and that I was able to achieve that without traveling from early March through the end of the year. This new work model is much more sustainable for me while not sacrificing my ability to service my clients.

And even though I was just as busy with client engagements as I was before, the lack of travel and the requirement to spend more time at home because of the coronavirus allotted me the time to finally write this book. I had been meaning to write a book related to my work with employee resource groups for the past five years, but I never really had the time. The pandemic provided me with the time necessary to finally not only write this book but to pen a second edition of my previous book *Auténtico: The Definitive Guide to Latino Career Success*, which I had cowritten with my dear friend Andrés Tapia.

Together, we have come to the end of the journey of laying out what it takes to achieve ERG excellence. We explored the current state of employee resource groups, cautioned against common derailers, and saluted those who take on the task of serving as an ERG leader. Next, we delved deeply into the 4C Model as holistic approach toward ERG excellence. The pillars of Career, Community, Culture, and Commerce were explored individually, as well as how they come together.

Finally, we looked at the importance of data and metrics in helping to capture the impact of employee resource groups. Outlined were the reasons that an effective measurement strategy helps an ERG determine its current state and track its progress, and also how metrics help an ERG better tell their story. We ended with the Google Maps analogy as it relates to effective strategic planning where ERGs first determine their current state and then define their desired future state before establishing their strategic plan.

But this book on ERG excellence was intended to be just the start of a new era. Building off the legacy of successful employee resource groups of both past and present, it is time to look at the next generation of employee resource groups in a new and disruptive way: ERGs that embrace metrics rather than hide from them. ERGs that see each of the 4C pillars as equals and knowing that over time they need to impact each. ERGs that are more inclusive than ever before in their embrace of allies and intersectionality. ERGs that know how to watch out for derailers that might knock them of their course. ERGs that are aligned more closely with organizational goals. And ERGs that are much more disciplined and strategic in their planning. These are the characteristics of the next generation of employee resource groups. These are the ERGs that will come the closest to achieving ERG excellence.

I close by sharing a proposed ERG Excellence Manifesto. This manifesto should serve as a published and public declaration of intentions for the next generation of employee resource groups. The manifesto is prescriptive in that it promotes new ideas for carrying out the things necessary to achieve ERG excellence. I encourage ERG members, diversity and inclusion practitioners, and those who believe in the power of ERGs to not only review this manifesto but to embrace it and to share it. ERG leaders and organizations that support employee resource groups – it's your turn.

The ERG Excellence Manifesto

1. *Organizations have failed to properly develop and recognize their ERG leaders*. They must shed the notion that ERG leaders can excel at their role without proper development. Instead, organizations should proactively address the development needs of ERG leaders via a systematic approach so that they reach

their true potential. Organizations also need to ensure ERG leaders' efforts and contributions are recognized via additional compensation, performance appraisal acknowledgment, or other ways to demonstration gratitude for the value they provide.

2. *ERGs must engage with and resolve common ERG derailers.* Every ERG will have their challenges, but without regularly checking to see if they are keeping common derailers at bay, an ERG cannot achieve excellence. ERG derailers can't be ignored and the sooner an ERG can address them, the more effective the employee resource group will be.
3. *ERGs must enhance the cultural competency within an organization to achieve diversity, equality, belonging, and inclusion goals.* ERGs that don't effectively impact the Culture pillar weaken the power of their group and their initiatives.
4. *Organizations must be willing to capitalize on all the talent that exists within employee resource groups.* Aligning ERGs with talent management will create more inclusive environments and equip organizations to leverage a workforce that will have an increasingly diverse identity.
5. *ERGs need to double down on the relentless pursuit of data analytics and metrics that matter.* Employee resource groups need to make more data-driven decisions, and they need to collect metrics that not only measure their activity but also quantify their impact. Doing so will help them tell their story and quiet ERG critics.
6. *ERGs must embrace their role as a talent engine for their organization with honorable intent.* Employee resource groups should seek to meet the professional development needs of individuals from various job levels through solid programming. Organizations should celebrate those ERGs who demonstrate this ambition because we all benefit.

7. *Every employee resource group must give back to the community.* True excellence requires leveraging high ERG achievement so that the broader community achieves success. The journey toward excellence is incomplete if ERGs don't give back to others.

8. *ERGs need to get over their ambivalence about being an underutilized business asset by aligning with organizational goals and redefining it on their own terms.* Where ambition is personal, alignment is collective. The impact of ERG power and influence is diluted if they do not support business goals. ERGs must contribute in a differentiated way than it has in years past.

9. *The next generation of employee resource groups can be more powerful by pursuing a holistic value proposition.* Resist mediocracy. Instead, develop an ERG that embraces and celebrates the 4C Model™ as a way to have a wide-ranging and transformational impact.

10. *Master strategic planning so you can chart a course toward excellence.* Master the ability to determine the current state of your ERG, so you can chart an accurate and appropriate course toward your desired future state.

ABOUT THE AUTHOR

Dr. Robert Rodriguez is the president of DRR Advisors LLC (www.drradvisors.com), a diversity consulting firm based in Chicago, IL. He is considered one of the nation's leading experts on employee resource groups and has worked with over 300 companies helping to elevate their ERG initiatives. He also has deep subject matter expertise in the area of Latino talent management.

Dr. Rodriguez is the creator of the 4C Model™, the most widely used ERG strategic framework in corporate America, as well the 4C ERG Assessment™, the only ERG diagnostic instrument on the market.

He holds a doctorate in Organization Development and previously held leadership roles at Target, 3M, BP Amoco and The Washington Post.

His previous two books include, "*Latino Talent: Effective Strategies to Recruit, Retain & Develop Hispanic Professionals*" (Wiley, 2008) and "*Auténtico: The Definitive Guide to Latino Career Success, 2nd Edition*" (Berrett-Koehler, 2021) co-written with Andrés Tapia.

INDEX